IT'S THE LORD'S SUPPER

The Eucharist of Christians

by
Lucien Deiss, C.S.Sp.

Translated by
Edmond Bonin

COLLINS

Collins Liturgical Publications
187 Piccadilly, London W1V 9DA

First published as *La Cène du Seigneur, Eucharistie des Chrétiens,* © 1975, Le
Centurion, Paris. English translation copyright © 1976 The Missionary Society
of St Paul the Apostle in the State of New York, USA.

Excerpts from *The Jerusalem Bible*, copyright © 1966 Darton, Longman & Todd
Ltd, and Doubleday & Company Inc. Reprinted by permission.

ISBN 0 00 599657 0

This edition first published 1980

Made and printed in Great Britain by
Fletcher & Son Ltd, Norwich

Contents

Introduction   1

I   The Riches of Tradition   5

The concluding of the covenant on Sinai (Exodus 24:1-11)   **6**
The new covenant, according to Jeremiah (31:31-34)   **9**
The accounts of the institution at the last supper   **11**
The breaking of bread   **13**
The bread of life, according to John 6   **17**
The Eucharistic prayer in the *Didache*   **22**
The testimony of Saint Justin   **25**
The *Apostolic Tradition* of Hippolytus of Rome   **28**

II   The Lord's Supper   33

On the first day of unleavened bread when the passover lamb
    was sacrificed   **33**
As they were eating (Matthew 26:26)   **36**
The last supper and the Jewish passover rite   **37**
Having given thanks   **39**
The covenant in my blood   **41**
The servant of Yahweh, "covenant of the people"   **42**
The universal covenant   **44**

III   The Eucharist as Thanksgiving   46

The word *eucharist*   **46**
Thanksgiving in Jewish piety   **48**
Paschal thanksgiving   **51**

IV   The Eucharist as Sacrifice   68

Sacrifice in general   **68**

Biblical sacrifices   71
Jesus' sacrifice at the last supper and on the cross   75
The sacrifice of the Mass   84
The Mass in our lives   91
The language of signs   96
The number and frequency of Masses   100

V   The Eucharist as Real Presence   104

The lesson of history   104
The glorified body of the risen Christ   110
The presence of Christ   114
The permanence of the real presence   123
Present-day investigations   131

VI   The Eucharist Today   137

Toward the feast of the resurrection   138
The celebration of Christ present in the Word   140
The celebration of Christ present in the Eucharist   145
Communion, a sharing of love   153

Introduction

According to the belief of the Church as set forth by Vatican II, the Mass is "the fount and apex of the whole Christian life," and the Eucharistic assembly constitutes the center of the ecclesial community.[1] Yet this center—the very heart of the Church—seems threatened now. Lack of faith in the real presence, discarding the traditional term *transubstantiation* for newer ones like *transignification* and *transfinalization*, downgrading the private Mass in favor of communal celebrations, emphasis on symbolism as sufficient to express the whole Eucharistic mystery—such is the litany of problems with which the encyclical *Mysterium fidei* denounced the errors of the day.[2] And the list could easily be lengthened: there is so much going on. Many, for example, depreciate or forget the notion of sacrifice, reduce the Eucharistic meal to a simple friendship meal, consider the tabernacle a mere "cupboard for the sick," replace the presidency of the priest by a lay ministry, and substitute profane texts for the Word of God or rice and tea for bread and wine.

---

[1]*Dogmatic Constitution on the Church*, 11; and *Decree on the Ministry and Life of Priests*, 5. All Vatican II documents are quoted from *The Documents of Vatican II*, edited by Walter M. Abbott, S.J., and Very Rev. Msgr. Joseph Gallagher (New York: Guild Press, America Press, Association Press, 1966).

[2]*Mysterium fidei*, 9-14. See *The Pope Speaks*, Vol. 10, No. 4 (1965), pp. 311-312.

Still, it would be unjust to think that everything was perfect in the past and that Eucharistic belief and practice went astray precisely in our time—on the occasion of the Council, for instance. The opposite is true. The Council developed and sometimes revived the traditional faith, and there is no denying that it has promoted a more authentic celebration. Today, as in the past, treasures of faith and adoration are amassed in each Eucharist. What do passing peripheral deviations weigh compared to the rock-firm faith of the entire people of God? When a community decides to live brotherly love more deeply (and that is the proper grace of the Eucharist), when a priest prepares his homily seriously every day so that it may reveal the true face of Christ, when the assembly has immediate access—without the barrier of Latin—to that living Word on which is founded the new covenant proclaimed at Mass, when priests bear witness to unity and charity by concelebrating instead of saying Mass in their separate corners, no one thinks of writing an encyclical on the subject. And yet it is the ordinary practice of the Church, without pomposity or triumphalism, which daily builds up the ecclesial community and nourishes its life.

The subject of this book could have been treated in various ways. Just as I have not chosen to diagnose all the contemporary deviations, so I have not chosen to catalog the answers to them; for the solution to today's problems would be ineffectual tomorrow, when new questions arise. Neither have I wished to elaborate a synthesis that might unify all the Eucharistic themes around one pivotal idea, since these themes clearly are not all equally important and since they still bear the scars of the great battles which marked the conscience of the Church in the days of Berengarius (eleventh century) and the Reformation (sixteenth century). Rather, I have simply tried to underline a few themes which strike me as essential if we are "to believe and understand"[3] today: the Eucharist is thanksgiving (Chapter III), sacrifice (Chapter IV) and presence (Chapter V). Such a

---

[3]"To Believe and Understand" is the name of the series in which Father Deiss' book appeared in France.—Translator.

procedure was made possible only by examining what Scripture tells us about the last supper (Chapter II) and reintegrating that information into the whole body of revelation (Chapter I). But I readily admit that, in another era and for other mentalities, a different procedure would have been possible.

* *

*

The word *Eucharist* means "thanksgiving." Amid the distress of mankind today, amid the whirlpools in the river of history which unceasingly toss us about and yet unceasingly carry us closer to God, this book would like to be a book of joy and hope.

I

The Riches of Tradition

No more than the other sacraments is the Eucharist a reality of grace whose significance we can determine for ourselves, on the basis of our own reflection upon God, the destiny of mankind or the symbolism of meals. Of course, the bread we present to God grew out of our earth, and our human hands kneaded the dough for it; but only the power of the Spirit can transform it into the body of the Lord. Similarly, God alone can teach us the significance of the Eucharist and help us understand its mystery. We must, therefore, humbly study what he reveals to us in his Word and follow his footprints, so to speak, particularly in the history of Israel, the special scene of his revelation. Jesus plainly states that the Eucharist is the "new" covenant in his blood. How, then, can we understand it except by referring to the covenant we call "old"? He likewise says, "Do this as a memorial of me." How can we "do this" again unless we know exactly what "this" is? We might add here that, of all the sacraments in the New Testament, the Eucharist is the most deeply rooted in the history of Israel because it refers to that reality which constituted the people of God: the covenant.

The biblical documents presented here concern the celebration of the covenant on Sinai; the prophecy of the new covenant, according to Jeremiah; the Lord's supper, which realizes this new covenant; the breaking of the bread, which shows us the Eucharistic practice of the early community; and, lastly, the discourse on the bread of life (John 6), which is the last New Testament document on our subject.

From Christian tradition we shall see the *Didache*, which presents the first "Eucharistic" prayer; the testimony of Justin, who, toward the year 150, gives us the first description of the Mass; and the *Apostolic Tradition* of Hippolytus of Rome (c. 215), which contains the first anaphora.

These extremely rich sources form the foundation for Christian belief concerning the Eucharist.

THE CONCLUDING OF THE COVENANT ON SINAI (Exodus 24:1-11)

Jesus' words at the last supper contain a quotation of Exodus 24:8: "*This is the blood of the Covenant* which Yahweh has concluded with you." The words come from that part of Exodus (24:1-11) which recounts the great feast of the covenant on Sinai. Exegetes detect in these verses an amalgam of two narratives:

—The first—and probably the more ancient—comprises verses 1a and 8-11. Moses is shown celebrating the covenant on the mountain, together with Aaron and seventy elders of Israel. (We omit verses 1b-2, a later addition which contradicts verses 10-11.)

—The second account, quoted at the second indention, comprises verses 3-8. Beyond doubt, it is more recent: the twelve standing-stones representing the twelve tribes suggest that the Israelites are already installed in Canaan. It seems to combine two parallel versions, a fact which would explain a certain amount of redundancy. Here, the covenant is celebrated at the foot of the mountain.

The covenant according to Exodus 24:1-11

> [1]To Moses [God] had said, "Come up to Yahweh, your-
> self and Aaron, Nadab and Abihu, and seventy of the elders
> of Israel . . ." [1b-2].
> [3]Moses went and told the people all the commands of
> Yahweh and all ordinances. In answer, all the people said
> with one voice, "We will observe all the commands that Yah-
> weh has decreed." [4]Moses put all the commands of Yahweh
> into writing, and early next morning he built an altar at the
> foot of the mountain, with twelve standing-stones for the
> twelve tribes of Israel. [5]Then he directed certain young Israel-
> ites to offer holocausts and to immolate bullocks to Yahweh
> as communion sacrifices. [6]Half of the blood Moses took up
> and put into basins, the other half he cast on the altar. [7]And
> taking the Book of the Covenant he read it to the listening
> people, and they said, "We will observe all that Yahweh has
> decreed; we will obey." [8]Then Moses took the blood and cast
> it towards the people. "This," he said, "is the blood of the
> Covenant that Yahweh has made with you, containing all
> these rules."
> [9]Moses went up with Aaron, Nadab and Abihu, and sev-
> enty elders of Israel. [10]They saw the God of Israel beneath
> whose feet there was, it seemed, a sapphire pavement pure as
> the heavens themselves. [11]He laid no hand on these notables
> of the sons of Israel: they gazed on God. They ate and they
> drank.

The account in Exodus 24:1-2, 9-11

Moses ascends the mountain with Aaron, Nadab and
Abihu. (The later priestly tradition—cf. Leviticus 10:1—iden-
tifies the last two as sons of Aaron.) With them go the seventy
elders, who are very important because, first of all, they represent the chosen people (cf. Numbers 11:16). But between the nations and himself, God has placed Israel, a priestly people, the
firstfruits of mankind. The seventy also represent the whole of
humanity, which, according to the genealogical list in Genesis
10, consists of seventy nations. Jewish tradition maintained that
the law of Sinai had been promulgated in seventy languages,
each people receiving God's law through the mediation of
Israel. From the very beginning, then, the covenant of Sinai was
open to universalism.

The text goes on to make an extraordinary statement: "They saw the God of Israel. . . . They gazed on God." Realizing that we cannot look upon God without dying, the author points out that this was not a face-to-face vision. Moses and his friends saw, not "the holy of holies" of the heavenly temple, but rather the sapphire pavement under God's feet. All the same, the covenant   like faith!   marks the beginning of the vision of God.

"They ate and they drank." This detail likewise is extremely important, for it indicates a true covenant meal. The nation was God's guest; it sat at his table.

The account in Exodus 24:3-8

This second text stresses two points:

The first concerns what may be called the "preaching of the covenant"; Moses reports God's words to the people (v. 3), puts them into writing (v. 4), and then proclaims "the Book of the Covenant" (v. 7). We might note that the phrase "Moses went and told the people all the commands of Yahweh" (v. 3) clearly recalls "God spoke all these words" (Exodus 20:1), which prefaces the decalogue. Consequently, the "words" of Yahweh in this passage are the decalogue, which elsewhere is called "the words of the Covenant—the Ten Words" (Exodus 34:28). The phrase "and all the ordinances" (v. 3) refers to the code of the covenant inserted between the decalogue and Exodus 24:1. The celebration of the Sinai covenant, therefore, was organically linked with the proclamation of God's Word and its acceptance by the people.

The second point concerns the sacrifice. The altar represents Yahweh himself; the standing-stones testify to the people's commitment and serve as a memorial (cf. Genesis 31:44-45). Moses sprinkles altar and people, thus signifying that God and people become "consanguineous relatives," form one same family, and share one same "soul"   that is, one same life. (According to Leviticus 17:14, blood represents life.)

Conclusion

The Sinai covenant prefigured the New Testament covenant. Taking it as a whole, the way Israelitic tradition could read and live it, we can bring out the following points:

—*The preaching of the covenant*—that is, the Word of God proclaimed by Moses and accepted by the people. This celebration of the Word constituted the covenant: "This is the blood of the Covenant that Yahweh has made with you, *containing all these rules*." To separate Word and Eucharist in the new covenant is not simply inadvertence, but error.

—*The sacrifice of the covenant*, which united God and his people in one same spiritual consanguinity. The "blood of the Covenant" created the family of the children of God.

—*The communion meal*, where the table companions were God's invited guests: "They gazed on God. *They ate and they drank*."

THE NEW COVENANT, ACCORDING TO JEREMIAH (31:31-34)

The covenant of the last supper is described as "new." Some like to think it is a covenant according to the spirit of the gospel as opposed to Jewish law and prophecy. But such an interpretation runs counter to reality; for the opposition lies, not between the Old Testament and the gospel, but between two mentalities, two spiritual attitudes. There can be an old-covenant attitude even in the New Testament, and a new-covenant attitude in the Old. This is the very situation envisioned in Jeremiah 31:31-34. For the concept of new covenant is found precisely in what we so incorrectly call the "Old Testament."

> [31]See, the days are coming—it is Yahweh who speaks— when I will make a new covenant with the House of Israel (and the House of Judah), [32]but not a covenant like the one I made with their ancestors on the day I took them by the hand to bring them out of the land of Egypt. They broke that cove-

nant of mine, so I had to show them who was master. It is
Yahweh who speaks. ³³No, this is the covenant I will make
with the House of Israel when those days arrive—it is Yahweh who speaks. Deep within them I will plant my Law, writing it on their hearts. Then I will be their God and they shall
be my people. ³⁴There will be no further need for neighbour
to try to teach neighbour, or brother to say to brother,
"Learn to know Yahweh!" No, they will all know me, the
least no less than the greatest—it is Yahweh who speaks—
since I will forgive their iniquity and never call their sin to
mind.

In popular piety, the covenant concluded with Moses was
to dominate the tumult of the centuries to come. Yet it is this
very covenant, haloed in the glory of Sinai, that Jeremiah attacks with unprecedented boldness, in the only passage in the
Hebrew Bible where there is question of a new covenant. Now,
the law will be engraved in man's heart, carried in his inmost
being, so that no one may forget it. Each will be taught directly
by God and will see his sins forgiven.

In fact, the desire for a new covenant was incised like a
wound in Israel's flesh. The phrase "I will be their God, and
they shall be my people," quoted by Jeremiah, was the ferment
that transformed the religion of Israel into a new covenant.
Indeed, it seems almost too new to be called a covenant at all—
that is, a juridical contract founded upon law and binding two
parties—for it is transformed into a unique relationship of love
that enchains God's tenderness to his chosen people. We can
conclude that Jeremiah is attacking not so much the old covenant as the juridical and legalistic character which constantly
threatened it. The Israelites may have felt that, in virtue of the
contract, their merits gave them an advantage over God. What
Jeremiah is denouncing is this mercantile religion, in which
grace became a due and love a transaction. He shatters the
juridical notion of alliance and transforms it into a relationship
of love.

Such are the spiritual summits toward which Jeremiah
sought to draw the community of promise at the close of the
seventh century, as the reforms of pious King Josiah (622)
ground to a halt and Chaldea's battering rams threatened the

throne of the kingdom of Judah. If today we understand that each Mass should be the sublime renewal of this new covenant according to Jeremiah; if we remember that religion, now as well as then, is always in danger of degenerating into ritualism, and ritualism into formalism; if we realize that it is sometimes reduced to a formality at which one must "assist" in order to be considered a "practicing Catholic," to a nuptial or funeral rite, and even to a simple religious ceremony in which "religious, civil and military authorities" take part on great occasions; if this is so, then we can easily see the urgent need for a new Jeremiah in our liturgy of today!

THE ACCOUNTS OF THE INSTITUTION AT THE LAST SUPPER

The accounts of the institution at the last supper have come down to us in four different versions: that of Matthew 26:26-28, that of Mark 14:22-24, that of Luke 22:19-20, and that of Paul in 1 Corinthians 11:23-25.

A simple glance shows that these accounts fall into two groups:

—*The Matthew-Mark group*. This group doubtlessly represents the tradition used in Palestinian circles. Its symmetrical phrasing and verbal rhythm were refined by liturgical use and thus bespeak a later date than the Luke-Paul group.

Mark's text does not flow naturally and has very obviously undergone alterations. For example, the disciples receive the cup and drink from it (v. 23), and only then does Jesus tell them it was his blood (v. 24). It therefore seems that verse 23 was wedged between verses 22 and 24. In that case, verses 22 and 24 would be an account of the last supper and verses 23 and 25 an account of the Jewish passover.

As for Matthew, he depends on the same source as Mark. In verse 27, he corrects verse 23 of Mark. In 28, he adds "for the forgiveness of sins." In 29, he changes "God" to "Father," as he habitually does throughout his gospel.

—*The Luke-Paul group*. This group bears witness to the

tradition in use in the Church of Antioch. We note that Paul, in a formula used in the rabbinical schools, is referring to an older tradition: "This is what I received from the Lord and in turn passed on to you" (1 Corinthians 11:23). Since Paul's sojourn in Corinth (Acts 18:1-18) extended from the end of the year 50 to the middle of 52, his testimony dates from the very first years of Christianity—from the 40's, according to some authors.

In Luke's text, two points should be brought out. The section comprising verses 15-18, with its characteristically Lukan vocabulary, is considered either an account of the Jewish passover or an ancient text of the last supper, here designated solely by the words spoken over the cup. As for verses 19b—starting from "which will be given"—and 20, they are omitted in several manuscripts (including Codex D, from the sixth century). Textual criticism does not permit us to ascertain whether we have here a mutilation of the original text or, rather, an addition by a scribe seeking to harmonize the text of this recension with the other traditions.

Which is the older tradition? Mark's Semitic original shows through more. Paul and Luke exhibit better Greek, yet it is only natural that the Antiochians should very soon have felt the need of Grecizing these texts for their Greek-language celebrations. All we can say is that each tradition may include elements which lie very close to the original.

If our intellectual curiosity remains somewhat unsatisfied and a few texts keep us locked out of inner gardens, that is because the keys to understanding must be sought elsewhere: in the hands of the community. Indeed, it is the community which celebrated the Eucharist instead of describing it in documents; it is the community which lived the Eucharist before analyzing its structure. Christ's command for reiteration, "Do this as a memorial of me," does not even appear in the Matthew-Mark tradition. Quite possibly, it was taken as a mere rubric; now, at a celebration, one does not read a rubric, one executes it. That is what the early community did by celebrating the last supper in "the breaking of bread."

THE BREAKING OF BREAD

In Palestinian speech, the expression *the breaking of bread* quite naturally designated either the fact of tearing bread, or the entire rite which opened the meal as the head of the family took bread and recited the blessing, then broke the bread and shared it. In the early Christian community, this expression took on a special religious significance, since the Lord had performed those same actions at the last supper. In certain pericopes, "the breaking of bread" can be synonymous with "Eucharist," and "to break bread" with "to celebrate the Eucharist." Such is the case in 1 Corinthians 10:16, where Paul says, "The bread that we break is a communion with the body of Christ." Elsewhere, the respect due to the texts does not permit us to determine with certitude whether they refer to the Eucharist properly so called or to the rite which opened a simple religious meal.

In my opinion, if we place the question of the breaking of bread in a strictly sacramental perspective—asking "Is it or is it not the sacramental renewal of the last supper?" or, in other words, "Is it what we call our 'Mass'?"—we turn up a blind alley. It is simpler to observe how the early community, not greatly preoccupied with our notion of sacramentality, lived it. There we discover great riches that shed precious light on our Eucharist.

The multiplication of the loaves according to the synoptics

The synoptics present two accounts of the multiplication of the loaves: the first in Matthew 14:15-21, Mark 6:35-44 and Luke 9:12-27 (pericopes which are close to John 6:3-15), and the second in Matthew 15:32-39 and Mark 8:1-10. This miracle foreshadowed the last supper, where Jesus would offer his followers the "true bread of heaven" (John 6:32). Here is the literal translation of the first account, according to Mark 6:41:

And having taken the five loaves . . .
having raised his eyes to heaven,
he said the blessing.

And *he broke the loaves*,
and he gave [them] to the disciples
to serve them to [the crowd].

The miracle occurred shortly before the feast of the passover (John 6:4). The guests were seated "in groups . . . in
squares of hundreds and fifties" (Mark 6:39) as if to celebrate
the passover and hear the homily. Jesus instructed them at
length (6:34); and the miraculous bread, distributed—like the
Eucharist—by the hands of the disciples, was the fruit of his
tenderness: "He saw a large crowd; and he took pity on them
because they were like sheep without a shepherd" (6:34).

For Jesus, breaking bread meant, first of all, sharing the
love which comes from God. In missionary terms, we would say
that, for a long time yet, the Church must multiply the bread of
earth for the hungry—that is, offer them her love, which satisfies like bread—before she can tell them about the Eucharist,
the bread of heaven.

The community of the Acts of the Apostles

The Acts of the Apostles presents three summaries (2:42-
47; 4:32-35; and 5:12-16) which, through somewhat idealized
formulas, depict the life of the early community. The first summary speaks of the breaking of bread in the following terms:

These remained faithful
to the teaching of the apostles, to the brotherhood,
to *the breaking of bread* and to the prayers (2:42).

In Acts, the verb *proskarterein*, which we translate "to
remain faithful," ordinarily denotes participation in a religious
act: in prayer (1:14 and 6:4), in temple worship (2:46), or in the
service of the Word (6:4). The four expressions which follow are
grouped in two's and describe the cultual life of the early community.

First of all, there was teaching—*didache*—the normal introduction to the breaking of bread. The most beautiful example of such teaching is furnished us by the community of Troas.

It had assembled on the first day of the week (that is, on Sunday) precisely to *break bread*. Paul spoke at length—"till the middle of the night," in fact: too long for young Eutychus, who fell asleep. (It was hot—Luke explains that a number of lamps had been lit in the upstairs room—and the young lad had sat on the windowsill to catch any breeze there might be.) He fell from the third story and was killed. Paul, who had not yet finished his *didache*, resurrected him on the spot, then *broke bread* and continued his instruction (Acts 20:7-11).

Secondly, Luke mentions *koinonia*, which we render by "communion" or "brotherhood." *Koinonia* designates the fact of having something in common *(koinos)*. (Paul, for instance, says that the Father calls us to *koinonia* with his Son; cf. 1 Corinthians 1:9.) This communion expresses itself quite naturally by sharing a common table or pooling all possessions. Thus, in his second summary, Luke explains: "The whole group of believers was united, heart and soul. . . . Everything they owned was held in common *[koina]*" (4:32; cf. 2:44). We should observe that the breaking of bread is an integral part of a community whose members are, so to speak, fused by one same love into one single heart, one single soul.

Lastly, Luke mentions *prayer*, something self-evident for a Christian community created for praise and adoration (2:46-47), and the *breaking of bread*. "In Judaism . . . 'breaking of bread' never refers to a whole meal but only (*a*) the action of tearing the bread, and (*b*) the rite with which the meal opened."[1] Since Luke clearly did not intend to have us admire the community for reciting grace faithfully and eating regularly, we are then led to take "the breaking of bread" as the technical term for the celebration of the Eucharist. This celebration could be held in connection with a meal of agape. In this summary (coming from a different source, however), Luke writes, "They went as a body to the Temple every day but met in their houses for the breaking of bread; they shared their food gladly and generously; they praised God" (2:46-47). Here Luke mentions faithfulness to the Temple, the breaking of bread in private

---

[1]J. Jeremias, *The Eucharistic Words of Jesus* (New York: Charles Scribner's Sons, 1966), pp. 119-120.

homes, meals, and the prayer of praise. It is possible that in the community at Corinth, on the occasion of the "Lord's supper" (1 Corinthians 11:20), the agape preceded the Eucharist.

The disciples from Emmaus (Luke 24:13-35)

The story of the disciples from Emmaus is well known: everyone remembers how Cleopas and his companion recognized Jesus at the breaking of bread (24:35). The account treats of the presence of the risen Lord in the midst of the community. Jesus seemed to have been snatched away from his followers in an abyss of suffering symbolized by the final rending on the cross. The disciples were on the verge of despair: "Our own hope had been that he would be the one to set Israel free" (24:21). And yet the community was not orphaned. Luke seems to be telling it, "You are walking with the risen Lord, and you do not recognize him! You are traveling with him, and you do not know it!" But how recognize him? Mary of Magdala, despite the tenderness of her love and the perspicacity of her feminine intuition, had not recognized her Rabboni and had mistaken him for the gardener. Nor had Peter succeeded any better in seeing him behind the features of the stranger roasting sardines over the fire early one morning (John 21:9). Luke proposes two criteria for recognizing Jesus. The first is Scripture. "Starting with Moses and going through all the prophets, throughout the scriptures" (24:27)—on every page of the Bible, therefore—we can discover the face of the risen Lord, and then our heart kindles with joy and love. The second criterion is brotherly love. What had Cleopas and his companion done? They had invited a stranger to share the bread of hospitality with them. And the stranger proved to be Jesus! Exchanging roles with them, he revealed himself as the leader of the community, broke bread and gave it to them! To make the Eucharist is to welcome the stranger, to walk along with him, to share the bread of hospitality with him, to offer him one's love: and Jesus becomes present. Thus is created the community of believers around the risen Lord.

It would be idle to inquire whether the bread Christ broke
was "Eucharistic" —that is, whether he was present in it sacramentally—since it was he, the Lord himself, who was sitting at
table with them and giving it to them.

Conclusion

Good sense compels us to acknowledge that in certain texts
—at least in Acts 2:42 and 20:7, 11—the breaking of bread designates the Eucharist. Everywhere else, this rite admirably un-
derlines the spiritual dimension of the Lord's supper.

THE BREAD OF LIFE, ACCORDING TO JOHN 6

John's gospel does not relate the institution of the Lord's
supper but, on the other hand, records a long discourse by Jesus
on the bread of life (6:32-71), presented in the synagogue at
Capernaum after the miraculous multiplication of the loaves.

In a purely "spiritualistic" (and somewhat antisacramen-
tary) interpretation, Jesus spoke solely of faith in his person;
eating his flesh and drinking his blood signified committing
oneself totally through faith—"coming to him" and "believing
in him," as the text says (6:35), affirming that "the son of
Joseph, whose father and mother we know" (v. 42), is bread
from heaven that confers an eternal life (v. 58). In a "realistic"
(and prosacramentary) interpretation, Jesus was talking about
the Eucharist throughout the entire discourse. Lastly, in a
middle-of-the-road interpretation, Jesus propounded two teachings, centered successively on faith and on the Eucharist.

The diversity of these interpretations shows both the riches
the text contains and the problem it poses. We could boil the
problem down to the following dilemma: either eating the flesh
and drinking the blood (v. 54) should be understood spiritually,
without reference to the sacrament, and then we must admit
that Jesus expressed himself badly, mystifying all those good
souls whose down-to-earth common sense made them take his

Tradition of Matthew and Mark

Matthew 26:26-29	Mark 14:22-25

26 Now as they were eating Jesus took some bread, and when he had said the blessing, he broke (it) and giving (it) to the disciples, he said: "Take, eat, this is my body."	22 And as they were eating he took some bread, and when he had said the blessing, he broke (it) and gave (it) to them, and said: "Take, this is my body."
27 And taking a cup, and giving thanks he gave it to them, saying: "Drink all of you from this, 28 for this is my blood, (the blood) of the covenant which is to be poured out for many for the forgiveness of sins.	23 And taking a cup and giving thanks, he gave it to them, and all drank from it, 24 and he said to them, "This is my blood, (the blood) of the covenant, which is to be poured out for many.
29 I tell you from now on I shall not drink from the fruit of this vine until this day when I will drink new (wine) with you in the kingdom of my Father."	25 Amen, I tell you, no more shall I drink from the fruit of this vine, until this day when I will drink new (wine) in the kingdom of God."

Tradition of Luke and Paul

Luke 22:15-20

15 And he said to them, "I have longed
   to eat this passover with you before I suffer;
16 because, I tell you, I shall not eat it again
   until it is fulfilled in the kingdom of God."
17 Then, taking a cup, he gave thanks and said,
   "Take this and share it among you,
18 because I tell you, from now on
   I shall not drink from the fruit of the vine
   until the kingdom of God has come."

Luke 22:19-20	1 Corinthians 11:23-26
	23 On the night that he was betrayed, the Lord Jesus took some bread,
19 And taking some bread, giving thanks, he broke (it) and gave (it) to them, saying,	24 and giving thanks he broke (it), and said,
"This is my body which is given for you; do this as a memorial of me."	"This is my body, which (is) for you; do this as a memorial of me."
20 He did the same with the cup after supper, saying:	He also did the same with the cup after supper, saying:
"This cup is the new covenant in my blood which is poured out for you.	25 "This cup is the new covenant in my blood.
	Whenever you drink it, do this as a memorial of me."
18 Because I tell you, from now on, I shall not drink from the fruit of the vine	
until the kingdom of God has come."	26 Every time you eat this bread and drink this cup, you are proclaiming the death of the Lord until he comes.

words at face value; or his speech should be understood as pertaining to the Eucharist, and then such demands—without further explanation and well before the institution of the Lord's supper—appear unreasonable. In either case, the discourse seems hardly credible, and therefore hardly evangelical, since revelation does not defy common sense.

Unquestionably, the solution to this problem consists in distinguishing between the different redactional levels within the discourse:

—There is what Jesus said in the synagogue at Capernaum. In the context of the Jewish passover (6:4), he had multiplied the messianic bread (vv. 5-15), which the manna in Exodus had prefigured (vv. 32-33). Then, like Wisdom, in Proverbs 9:5, he invited men to eat the bread of his feast, the true bread from heaven that gives life to the world (v. 33). To eat this bread is to believe in his mission, which brings eternal life. "I am the bread of life. He who comes to me will never be hungry; he who believes in me will never thirst (v. 35). This statement sums up his whole utterance and can witness to the earliest level of the discourse.

—There is what John—or, rather, the redactor of the Johannine tradition—reported from this discourse. Besides giving it form and physiognomy, he put his own vocabulary and syntax as well as his doctrinal preoccupations in Jesus' mouth, thus illuminating and precising the discourse most specifically with reference to the Eucharist. As a matter of fact, if the final redaction of John's gospel can reasonably be placed toward the end of the first century (about 95?), there was then a span of some seventy years between what Jesus said at Capernaum and what we read in John 6. During that time, the community continued celebrating the Eucharist and meditating on the Lord's words. In all likelihood, it read the early text through the prism of its Eucharistic faith and enriched it with sacramental allusions.

—We must make particular mention of 6:51-58, indubitably the most clearly Eucharistic passage of all. Both the structure and the sense of verse 51 contain a direct allusion to the words of institution:

John 6:51	*1 Corinthians 11:24*
The bread that I shall give is my flesh for the life of the world.	This is my body, which is for you.

Verses 52-58 can be read as a Eucharistic homily showing how the early community "proclaimed the death of the Lord" (1 Corinthians 11:26). This whole section, 6:51-58, was doubtlessly inserted in the early narrative of John 6 at another redactional level.

Regardless of insertions and additions, John 6 as a whole, even if not historical—that is, even if not spoken by Jesus as it stands—remains fully authentic; that is to say, it belongs authentically to the Word of God inspired by the Spirit. This influence of the community on the text reminds us that the Christian faith—including faith in the Eucharist—is based not on a text, whatever its historicity and authenticity, but primarily on the faith of the early ecclesial community. We are not the "children" of a book, though it be named "gospel," but the heirs of a community which celebrated the Eucharist before transcribing the memoirs of its faith on dead parchment.

Multiple themes, like a star shower, flash through the discourse on the bread of life. Let us focus on two of them. First, there is the relation between faith and sacrament, or, more exactly, the primacy of faith in the sacramental domain. Theologians constantly stress the efficacy of the sacrament operating in virtue of its own dynamism *(ex opere operato)*, and the intensive practice of frequent communion has perhaps fostered the belief that the ideal is to receive as often as possible. John 6 stands in opposition to all deviations in this matter. The Eucharist is preeminently the sacrament of faith. What counts is, not sacramental "overfeeding," but rather the total commitment to Christ Jesus that each communion should signify and promote: "Lord, who shall we go to? You have the message of eternal life." In this connection, authors note that the numerous

defections after the Eucharistic discourse foreshadowed Judas'
betrayal at the last supper; but Peter's faith was a prophecy of
all those who today repeat with him, "We believe; we know that
you are the Holy One of God" (cf. vv. 67-71).

Secondly, I would like to emphasize the relationship between the Eucharist and the incarnation. Where Paul and the
synoptics establish a link between the Lord's supper and his
passion and parousia, John further stresses its link with the incarnation. The most stupendous statement in this regard is surely the one in verse 57: "As I, whom am sent by the living Father, myself draw life from the Father, so whoever eats me will
draw life from me." The Eucharist is the sacrament of the incarnation. It communicates to the faithful the very life which
the Son has from the Father, and, consequently, delegates them
to the same mission. No mere loving tryst alone with Jesus, it
plunges each believer into the vast, swirling flood of the incarnation "to do the works that God wants" (6:28).

One last remark. Even today, a reader may be repelled by
the crudity of the expressions "eating the flesh" and "drinking
the blood." But they appear precisely in the section comprising
verses 51-58 and, for that reason, were doubtlessly not used by
Jesus. At any rate, in matters of biblical diction, one may
always choose what seems most suitable. Hence, we prefer to
speak of "eating the bread from heaven" or "drinking the cup
of blessing," expressions which are fully as biblical and universally accessible.

THE EUCHARISTIC PRAYER IN THE *DIDACHE*

In 1875, Philotheus Bryennios, the Orthodox Metropolitan
of Nicomedia, discovered in the convent of the Holy Sepulchre
in Constantinople a Greek manuscript containing, among other
documents, the *Didache* (= instruction) *of the Lord to the Hea-
then by the Twelve Apostles*. This work juxtaposes texts from
different periods and sources. Some of them may date back to
the 50's, like this "Eucharistic" prayer, the most venerable in
Christian antiquity:

As for the Eucharist, give thanks like this:

First, for the cup:

We give thee thanks, our Father,
for the holy vine of David thy servant
that thou hast revealed to us through Jesus, thy Child.
　　Glory to thee for ever!

Next, for the broken bread:

We give thee thanks, our Father,
for the life and the knowledge
that thou hast revealed to us through Jesus, thy Child.
　　Glory to thee for ever!

Just as this bread which we break,
once scattered over the hills,
has been gathered and made one,
so may thy Church too be assembled
from the ends of the earth into thy kingdom!
For glory and power are thine for ever.

No one is to eat or drink your Eucharist
except those who have been baptized in the name of the Lord;
for in this regard the Lord said:
"Do not give holy things to the dogs."

After you have eaten your fill, give thanks like this:

We give thee thanks, O holy Father,
for thy holy name
which thou hast made to dwell in our hearts,
for the knowledge, faith and immortality
that thou hast revealed to us through Jesus, thy Child.
　　Glory to thee for ever!

It is thou, almighty Master, who hast created the world,
that thy name may be praised;
for their enjoyment thou hast given
food and drink to the children of men;
but us thou hast graciously favoured
with a spiritual food
and with drink what gives eternal life, through Jesus, thy
　　Child.

Above all, we give thee thanks
for thine own great power.
    Glory to thee for ever!
    Amen.

Remember, Lord, thy Church,
to deliver her from all evil,
to make her perfect in thy love.
Gather her from the four winds,
this Church thou hast sanctified,
into the kingdom thou hast prepared for her.
For power and glory are thine for ever.
    Amen.

May the Lord come and may this world pass away!
    Amen.
Hosanna to the house of David!
He who is holy, let him approach.
He who is not, let him do penance.
    Marana tha!
    Amen.[2]

This prayer is the golden link which binds Jewish prayer to
the Christian Eucharist. From Israelitic tradition it retains the
blessing over the cup, then over the bread, and the closing triple
blessing punctuated by the acclamation "Glory to thee for
ever!" The community which used this prayer was still very
close to Judaism but Christianized the traditional formula by
adding the phrase "through Jesus, thy Child." Its meal opened
on to the Lord's supper (as shown by the invitation "He who is
holy, let him approach") and, in my opinion, surely included it.
Granted that we do not find the account of the institution there,
but we may reasonably assume that a community which met to
celebrate the Lord's supper had no need of repeating to itself
what it was doing.

Welling up from the Jewish soul turned Christian, this
prayer brims over with praise and thanksgiving and fairly
shouts its expectation of the Lord. On reading it, we can sense

---

[2]L. Deiss, *Early Sources of the Liturgy* (Staten Island: Alba House, 1967), pp.
13-16.

the joy, the blessing, the lyricism, too, of a community celebrating the Lord's supper as it awaited his return—in a word, everything which so many centuries of rubrical habits have made us lose and which today's liturgy is trying to rediscover!

THE TESTIMONY OF SAINT JUSTIN

Justin was born in the heart of Galilee, at Flavia Neapolis (Sichem), not far from the well where Jesus had promised the Samaritan woman living water. A peripatetic philosopher, he became a Christian about 130. Some twenty years later, he addressed to the Emperor Antoninus Pius two *Apologies* in which he expounds the Christian faith and, in the process, tells us about the Eucharist. The dedication of the work is of a splendid loftiness and audacity: "To the Emperor Antoninus Pius . . . and to the whole Roman people, I address this discourse and petition for men of every race who are unjustly hated and persecuted, I who am one of them, Justin, son of Priscus, son of Baccheius, a native of Flavia Neapolis in Palestine." Justin knew that the Christians were being condemned simply because they bore that name, and yet he wrote, "I who am one of them." Such a testimony is credible. He signed it in his blood by dying a martyr toward 165, thus confirming what he had written in his *Apology*: "Nobody believed in Socrates deeply enough to die for his teaching. . . . But for Christ, not only philosophers and men of letters, but even artisans and uneducated men have made light of fame, fear and death."[3]

The baptismal Mass, around 150

The communal prayers

As for us, after the one who believes and has given his assent has been purified, we lead him to the place where those who are called the "brethren" are assembled.

---

[3]*Apology II*, 80, in Deiss, *op. cit.*, pp. 20-21.

We pray fervently together for ourselves, for him who
has just been enlightened, and for all the rest in whatever
place they may be, that, having come to know the truth, we
may be judged worthy to practise good works, keep the com-
mandments and so obtain everlasting salvation.

The kiss of peace

When the prayers are finished, we give each other the
kiss [of peace].

Anaphora[4]

Then bread and a cup of wine to which water has been
added are brought to the one who is presiding over the assembly of the brethren.

He takes them, gives praise and glory to the Father of
the universe, through the name of the Son and of the Holy
Spirit, and then makes a long eucharist, for having been
judged worthy of these good things.

When he has finished, all the people present acclaim it
saying: "Amen." Amen is a Hebrew word which means: so be
it.

Communion

When the president has finished the eucharist and all the
people have acclaimed it, those whom we call deacons distrib-
ute the consecrated bread, and water and wine, to each of
those who are present and take some away to those who are
not.

We call this food "Eucharist." No one can have a share
in it unless he has undergone the washing which forgives sins

---

[4]*Anaphora:* a Greek word meaning "elevation" and, in ancient liturgies, designating the prayers from the dialogue of the preface to the *Amen* which concludes the canon. Traditionally, the anaphora comprises the dialogue of the
preface, the thanksgiving, the account of the institution, the anamnesis, the
epiclesis and the doxology.

Anamnesis: a Greek word meaning "remembrance" and commemorating the
mysteries of Christ. (Our missals usually call this "the memorial prayer."—
Translator.)

Epiclesis: a Greek word meaning "invocation" and designating the prayer
which invokes the coming of the Holy Spirit upon the bread and the wine of the
Eucharist.

and regenerates, and unless he lives according to the teaching of Christ. For we do not take this food as though it were ordinary bread and wine. But, just as through the Word of God Jesus Christ became incarnate, took flesh and blood for our salvation, in the same way this food, which has become Eucharist thanks to the prayer formed out of the words of Christ, and which nourishes and is assimilated into our flesh and blood, is the flesh and blood of incarnate Jesus: this is the doctrine that we have received.

For indeed the Apostles, in those memoirs of theirs which are called "Gospels," tell us that Jesus gave them this command: having taken bread, he gave thanks and said: "Do this in memory of me, this is my body"; in the same way, having taken the cup, he gave thanks and said: "This is my blood." And it was to them alone that he gave them.[5]

The liturgy of the Lord's day

A community of charity and prayer

Those who are well-to-do come to the help of those who are in need, and we always lend one another assistance.

In all that we offer, we bless the Creator of the universe through his Son Jesus Christ and through the Holy Spirit.

The celebration of the Lord's day

On the day which is called Sun-day, all, whether they live in the town or in the country, gather in the same place.

Then the Memoirs of the Apostles or the Writings of the Prophets are read for as long as time allows.

When the reader has finished, the president speaks, exhorting us to live by these noble teachings.

Then we all rise together and pray.

Then, as we said earlier, when the prayer is finished, bread, wine and water are brought. The president then prays and gives thanks as well as he can. And all the people reply with the acclamation: Amen!

After this the eucharists are distributed and shared out to everyone, and the deacons are sent to take them to those who are absent.[6]

---

[5] *Apology I*, 65-66, in Deiss, *op. cit.*, pp. 23-26.

[6] *Apology I*, 67, *ibid.*

The Mass as described by Saint Justin exhibits the essential elements of the Christian celebration:

The celebration of the Word

—Reading, "for as long as time allows," of the gospels (also called the "Memoirs of the Apostles") or the "Writings of the Prophets."
—Homily by the president.
—Prayers for the community and for the universal Church.
—The kiss of peace, before the anaphora.

The celebration of the Eucharist

—Presentation of the offerings: bread, wine and water.
—Eucharistic prayers by the president. "He gives praise and glory to the Father of the universe, through the name of the Son and of the Holy Spirit." The bread and the wine become the body and the blood of Christ. The style of this prayer remains very free: the president gives thanks "as well as he can."
—Acclamation by the people: Amen!
—Communion. The "eucharists" are distributed to the community, and the deacons take some to absent members.

THE *APOSTOLIC TRADITION* OF HIPPOLYTUS OF ROME (about 215)

About 1551, there was unearthed in the Roman cemetery of Agro Verano on the Tiburtine Way a statue of Hippolytus of Rome, on the plinth of which was engraved a list of his works. Among other titles was *[Ap]ostolike Paradosis*, that is, *Apostolic Tradition*. This work proved to be an unbelievable breakthrough, for it offers us the first text of an anaphora.

Hippolytus' life was anything but dull. A priest of the

Church of Rome, combining the prestige of immense erudition with real literary talent, he unfortunately decided to assail Pope Zephyrinus (198-217) and have himself elected antipope. He was temporarily kept from carrying out his scheme, however, by the impiety of the emperor in unleashing a persecution. Before long, another emperor, Maximinus the Thracian (235-238), issued an edict proscribing all Church leaders guilty of having taught the gospel. As a result, pope and antipope, Pontian and Hippolytus, were brought together in a deportation camp—in those days, the mines of Sardinia—where their common suffering and misery opened the door to reconciliation. Both died as martyrs on "the island of death." Pope Fabian (236-250) had their bodies brought back to Rome, and their funerals were held on the same day, August 13, in the year 236 or 237.

The *Apostolic Tradition* is a liturgical compilation dating from approximately 215. In discussing the consecration of a bishop, Hippolytus presents the Eucharistic prayer from the consecratory Mass:

Acclamation

Let the deacons present the offering [to the bishop]. When he lays his hands on it, with the whole college of priests, let him say the words of thanksgiving:
—The Lord be with you.
—And with thy spirit.
—Let us lift up our hearts.
—They are turned to the Lord.
—Let us give thanks to the Lord.
—It is worthy and just.

Thanksgiving

Let him continue thus:

We give thee thanks, O God,
through thy beloved Child, Jesus Christ,
whom thou hast sent to us in the last times
as Saviour, Redeemer and Messenger of thy will.
He is thine inseparable Word
through whom thou hast created all things
and in whom thou art well pleased.

Thou didst send him from heaven
into the womb of a Virgin.
He was conceived and became incarnate,
he manifested himself as thy Son,
born of the Spirit and the Virgin.

He accomplished thy will
and, to acquire a holy people for thee,
he stretched out his hands while he suffered
to deliver from suffering
those who believe in thee.

Account of the Institution

When he gave himself up willingly to suffering
to destroy death,
to break the fetters of the devil,
to trample hell under his feet,
to spread his light abroad over the just,
to establish the Covenant
and manifest his Resurrection,
he took bread,
he gave thee thanks and said:
"Take, eat, this is my body
which is broken for you."
Likewise for the chalice, he said:
"This is my blood
which is poured out for you.
When you do this,
do it in memory of me."

Anamnesis

We then, remembering thy death
and thy Resurrection,
offer thee bread and wine,
we give thee thanks for having judged us worthy
to stand before thee and serve thee.

Epiclesis

And we beg thee
to send thy Holy Spirit
upon the offering of thy holy Church,
to gather and unite
all those who receive it.

May they be filled with the Holy Spirit
who strengthens their faith in the truth.
So may we be able to praise and glorify thee
through thy Child, Jesus Christ.

Doxology

Through him, glory to thee, and honour,
to the Father and to the Son, with the Holy Spirit,
in thy holy Church,
now and for ever.
    Amen.[7]

Though not the sole formula of the Roman Mass, the formula Hippolytus presents does afford us one particularly precious testimony concerning it—the only one we have from those remote days when our present liturgy was fashioned. First and foremost, it evinces the freedom which still existed in the Roman liturgy at that time to improvise the Eucharistic prayer. Accordingly, Hippolytus presents his text, not as a fixed formula, but simply as a model:

> Let the bishop give thanks in the manner described above. It is not, however, necessary for him to use the form of words set out there, as though he had to make the effort to say them by heart in his thanksgiving to God.
> Let each man pray according to his abilities. If a man can make a becoming and worthy prayer, it is well. But if he prays in a different way, and yet with moderation, you must not prevent him, provided that the prayer is correct and conforms to orthodoxy.[8]

We should note the perfect purity of structure in this prayer. Uninterrupted by the *Sanctus*, the preface leads directly into the account of the institution, which closes with the anamnesis, the epiclesis, and the doxology. We can well understand why tradition seized upon this masterpiece of simplicity and spread its influence far and wide. The original Greek—now lost

---

[7]In Deiss, *op. cit.*, pp. 38-41.

[8]*Apostolic Tradition*, 9, in Deiss, *op. cit.*, p. 49.

—was translated into Arabic, Syriac, Sahidic and Bohairic Coptic (dialects of Upper and Lower Egypt), and Latin. Even today, the old Roman prayer composed in Greek is still recited on African soil by Ethiopian priests. And, after forgetting him for almost fifteen centuries, the Roman rite Church has finally remembered Hippolytus and used his prayer as the basis of Eucharistic Prayer II.

II

The Lord's Supper

The starting point for any reflection upon the Eucharist must always be the Lord's enjoinder, "Do this as a memorial of me." Our most urgent task, then, is to determine what is meant by "this." What did Jesus do at the last supper?

ON THE FIRST DAY OF UNLEAVENED BREAD, WHEN THE PASSOVER LAMB WAS SACRIFICED

The triple synoptic tradition (Matthew 26:17-19; Mark 14:12-16; Luke 22:7-13) prefaces the last supper with an account of the preparations for the paschal meal: "On the first day of Unleavened Bread, when the Passover lamb was sacrificed, his disciples said to him, 'Where do you want us to go and make the preparations for you to eat the passover?' " (Mark 14:12). In the mind of the evangelists, therefore, the last supper was celebrated in the context of the Jewish passover. Now, this context

was the richest Israel could offer for celebrating the new covenant in the death and resurrection of Jesus.

In the course of Israel's history, several feasts had coa-
lesced to constitute the paschal solemnity. The passover seems
to have originated as a pastoral festival incorporated into a no-
madic or seminomadic life style. It included the sacrificing of a
yearling lamb in order to obtain prosperity and fertility for the
flock. Come springtime, it doubtlessly marked the moving of
the livestock to mountain pastures. The blood smeared upon the
doorposts was meant to ward off malefic powers, the "destroying angel." Then, too, within the agricultural framework of a
sedentarized life, there was the feast of unleavened bread (Leviticus 23:5-8), which marked the beginning of the barley harvest,
"the time you begin to put your sickle into the standing corn"
(Deuteronomy 16:9). Doubtlessly of Canaanite origin, it was
adopted by the Israelites once they had settled in Canaan. Certain sources (cf. Exodus 34:18 and 25; 12:1-14 and 15-20) draw
a sharp distinction between these two feasts—that of the passover and that of unleavened bread; but since both were celebrated in the springtime, they readily fused into one, perhaps
after Josiah's reform in 622. Finally, there was what we might
call a historicization of these feasts. For Israel celebrated the
springtime of its birth as well: a decisive historic intervention by
God on its behalf, an intervention sublimated in the image of
the liberation from Egypt. The Bible preserved only vestiges of
the prehistory of these three feasts, and the weight of the centuries eventually blended into a single solemn celebration the
passover, the feast of unleavened bread, and the exodus from
Egypt (cf. Exodus 12:1-28; Deuteronomy 16:1-8).

Though the history of the passover remains somewhat
hazy, its spiritual significance shines with intense light. To describe this liberation, Israel exhausted the vocabulary of human
tenderness. In its mind, liberation from Egypt was like a mysterious birth, with God taking it in his arms as a father takes his
newborn child (Hosea 11:1-3). God "adopted" this people in the
wilds of the howling desert (Deuteronomy 32:10); there, the
young maiden Israel was wed to her God (Jeremiah 2:2); and
there she was loved "with an everlasting love" (Jeremiah 31:3).

At this point, I must quote the *Poem of the Four Nights*, which is certified in the targum and aptly conveys the meaning of the paschal feast in Christ's day:

> This is a night for keeping vigil, the night predestined for redemption in the name of Yahweh as the children of Israel came forth from Egypt, liberated. But the *Book of Memoirs* contains four nights.
> The first, when Yahweh manifested himself to create the earth. Now, the earth was a shapeless void, and darkness was spread over the deep. And the Word of Yahweh was the Light, and it shone. And he called it "First Night."
> The second, when Yahweh appeared to Abraham. . . . And he called it "Second Night."
> The third, when Yahweh appeared to the Egyptians, in the middle of the night. . . . His right hand protected the firstborn of Israel, so that the Scripture might be fulfilled: "Israel is my firstborn son" (Exodus 4:22). And he called it "Third Night."
> The fourth, when the world comes to an end in order to be redeemed. The yokes of iron will be broken, and the perverse generations annihilated; Moses will arise from the midst of the desert, and the Messiah King will come from on high. . . . This is the night of the passover for the name of Yahweh, the night set apart and appointed for the redemption of all the generations of Israel.[1]

The passover, therefore, was at one and the same time a memorial of creation, of that night from which God caused the earth to spring forth unto the glory of his name; a memorial of Abraham's sacrifice—the feast of the love of this patriarch "who did not refuse his son, his only son" (cf. Genesis 22:12); a memorial of the deliverance from Egypt, when God, freeing Israel from the fetters of captivity, declared, "Israel is my first-born son" (Exodus 4:22); and, finally, a prophecy of the last day, when his glory will invade earth for eternity. The nocturnal festival of the four nights celebrated the essence of Israel's religion. In Christ's day, the passover was "the feast" (Matthew 26:5) *par excellence*. The liberation from Egypt stood as the

---

[1]See *Neophyti I*, Vol. 2 (Madrid-Barcelona, 1970), pp. 312-313.—The targum is the Aramaic version of the Hebrew Bible for use in the liturgy of the synagogue.

archetype of all liberations. Jewish tradition as presented in the *Mishnah* comments thus: "[God] has led us from bondage to freedom, from sadness to joy, from mourning to feasting, from darkness to brilliant light, from servitude to redemption. Let us, therefore, sing *Alleluia* before him" (*Pesahim*, V, 5).

AS THEY WERE EATING
(Matthew 26:26)

The Eucharist was instituted during the paschal meal.

In biblical lands, eating at the same table was a special token of friendship: sharing the same bread meant sharing the same love. To sunder the fellowship ratified at a meal was a particularly odious betrayal, as in the case of Judas, of whom it was written: "Someone who shares my table rebels against me" (Psalm 41:10 = John 13:18).

It is well to remember, also, that this paschal meal was a covenant meal—and an altogether special one, since, for Jesus and the Twelve, it was also a farewell meal. Still, it fit into the long chain of communion meals which—from Sinai, where "they ate and they drank" (Exodus 24:11), through the countless covenant meals in the course of Israel's history, through those Jesus shared with his apostles before and after the resurrection, down to the celebrations of the breaking of bread in the early community—introduce man into the eternal banquet.

Nor can this farewell meal be separated from the other meals in Jesus' public life, which were a proclamation in act of his "good news." When accepting bread one day, Jesus asserted, "I did not come to call the virtuous, but sinners" (Matthew 9:13). When receiving the repentant woman at table and letting her wash his feet with her tears and dry them with her hair, he signified that he was welcoming her into the family of those who had found forgiveness and peace (Luke 7:49-50). When multiplying the loaves and fishes for the famished in the "lonely place" where he had healed their sick, he multiplied joy for that feast of the poor (Matthew 14:15-21). When he sat at Zacchaeus' table, he proclaimed, "The Son of Man has come to seek out and save what was lost" (Luke 19:9-10). And the Pharisees, for their part, when they accused him of eating with sinners (Mark 2:16), merely established who belongs to Jesus' family: those who willingly acknowledge their sinfulness, precisely to be saved. The bread he broke with sinners clearly announced the Eucharistic meal in which the wine would be poured out "for the forgiveness of sins" (Matthew 26:28).

THE LAST SUPPER AND THE JEWISH PASSOVER RITE

We know at least the essential outlines of the Jewish passover ritual, out of which the Lord's supper grew.

Entrance rite

The celebration opened with a blessing of the feast and of the wine (first cup); with a purification rite, which Christ undoubtedly amplified when he washed the apostles' feet and delivered his catechesis (John 13:2-15; cf. Luke 22:24-27) and, finally, with the eating of the bitter herbs—probably the point at which Jesus announced Judas' betrayal (Matthew 26:20-25; Mark 14:17-21; Luke 22:21-23) and gave him the piece of bread (John 13:21-30).

Homily and prayers

We may consider this part a liturgy of the Word, designed to underscore the meaning of the feast. At the request of one of those at table, the father of the family, drawing upon popular exegesis, used to bring out the significance of certain elements: the term *passover*, for instance, meant "passing," for Yahweh "passed over the houses of the sons of Israel in Egypt" (Exodus 12:27); the bread lacked yeast, for, in their haste to depart, "the people carried off their dough, still unleavened" (Exodus 12:34); the paschal lamb recalled the first passover sacrifice, whose blood protected the Israelites' houses from the destroying angel (Exodus 12:21-23); and, lastly, the bitter herbs conjured up the bitterness of captivity. That is the context in which Jesus uttered the discourse reported in John 14-17. We may read it both as Jesus' farewell speech and as his paschal homily to his Church. This part of the ceremony concluded with everyone praying the first section of the Hallel (Psalm 113 or 113-114).

Passover meal

Here was the heart of the celebration. It comprised a second purification rite, the father's blessing over the bread he broke, the eating of the paschal lamb, and, after the meal, the blessing of the third cup, called also "the blessing-cup" (1 Corinthians 10:16). This is where Jesus' consecratory words were spoken over the bread before the eating of the paschal lamb, and over the wine "after supper" (Luke 22:20; 1 Corinthians 11:25).

Conclusion

The meal ended with the last part of the Hallel, Psalms 114-118 (or 115-118), which Jesus sang with his disciples, as we learn from Matthew 26:30 and Mark 14:26.

Outlining gives us the following chart:

The Jewish passover rite	*The Lord's supper*
A) Entrance rite	
—Blessing of the feast and of the first cup.	
—Purification rite (ablution).	Washing of the feet, and catechesis (John 13:2-15; cf. Luke 22:24-27).
—Eating of the bitter herbs.	Announcement of Judas' betrayal (?).

B) *Homily and prayers*

—Pesach haggadah by the father, in   Jesus' discourse (John 14-17).
  Aramaic.
—First part of the Hallel (Psalm
  113 or 113-114), in Hebrew.
—Second cup (cup of the haggadah).

C) *Passover meal*

—Purification rite (ablution).
—Blessing by the father over   Jesus' words over the bread: "This
  the bread.   is my body . . ."
—Eating of the paschal lamb.
—Third cup (cup of blessing).   Jesus' words over the wine: "This
                                        is my blood . . ."

D) *Conclusion*

—Second part of the Hallel (Psalms   Singing of the psalms (Matthew
  114-118 or 115-118), in Hebrew.   26:30;   Mark 14:26).
—Fourth cup (?).

The text of the institution has, therefore, been somewhat condensed. In particular, the elements of the Jewish passover rite have disappeared, doubtlessly because they were deemed sufficiently familiar to Jewish circles and also because the Christians newly converted from paganism were more concerned with the Christian celebration of the Lord's supper.

At this point, one conclusion is already inescapable. The Mass is indeed a meal, but not an ordinary one at which bread and wine are consecrated; rather, it is a festive meal within a liturgy of prayer and especially of thanksgiving (cf. the Hallel). Doing "this" in memory of Jesus means, not merely eating together, but also and at the same time rendering thanks for the liberation of the Christian exodus, the passover of Jesus.

HAVING GIVEN THANKS . . .

In Israel, meals always took on a certain religious character. The host would recite this blessing over the bread: "Blessed

be you, Yahweh our God, King of the universe, who draw bread
from the earth." And over the wine: "Blessed be you, Yahweh
our Lord, King of the universe, who create the fruit of the
vine." These blessings—which the new liturgy of the Mass has
once again adopted for the presentation of the bread and wine—
implied that the guests not only declared themselves friends
before God but, in presenting their friendship to him, also
blessed him together. Their common meal became common
prayer. When the Pharisees accused Jesus of going so far as to
eat with publicans, they were implicitly upbraiding him for con-
stituting a community of prayer with them.

The evangelists expressly note that Jesus said the blessing
(Matthew-Mark), that he gave thanks (Luke-Paul). In the blessings for the feast, we must surely include the one which was
joined to that of the cup and which read thus: "Blessed be you,
Yahweh our God, King of the universe, who give your people
Israel this feast of unleavened bread, for their joy and as a memorial. Blessed be you who sanctify Israel and its times."
Though the synoptic tradition has not preserved Jesus' "Eucharistic" prayers for us, we know he had such a unique and
personal way of giving thanks that the disciples from Emmaus
were able to recognize him "at the breaking of bread" (Luke
24:35). When he spoke to God, his prayer suggested a tenderness and closeness as deep and warm as that of any son for
his father. He liked to call him "Abba" ("Father"). Unique in
the literature of the period, this title was "a children's word,
used in everyday talk"[2]—a little like our "papa"—while yet
carrying overtones of reverence and submission: "Abba (Father)! Everything is possible for you. . . . But let it be as you,
not I, would have it" (Mark 14:36). He wanted this title to be
given to no one else on earth (Matthew 23:9). At prayer, he
would also raise his eyes to heaven and begin with these words:
"I bless you, Father," as in the hymn of jubilation (Matthew
11:25); or again: "Father, I thank you for hearing my prayer. I
knew indeed that you always hear me," as before Lazarus'

---

[2]J. Jeremias, *New Testament Theology* (New York: Charles Scribner's Sons,
1971), p. 67.

tomb (John 11:41-42). The long prayer which closes the discourse after the last supper (John 17), and in which praise and love are reflected in the divine eternity (cf. 17:5, 23), is the mirror of Jesus' "Eucharistic" soul.

THE COVENANT IN MY BLOOD

Jesus clearly announced his imminent death and set it in relation to the last supper. As a matter of fact, he spoke of his body which would be "given" for his followers, and his blood which would be "poured out" for sins. Just as bread is broken to be shared among brothers, so his body would be torn by suffering when offered in sacrifice; just as wine flows like "the blood of the grape" (Genesis 49:11), so his blood would stream from his body in the press of the passion.

This death was related to the covenant. In biblical lands, concluding a covenant usually entailed immolating a victim whose blood became "the blood of the covenant." Thus, on Sinai, Moses sprinkled both altar and people with the blood of one same victim to signify the union—similar to that of a family united by the same blood—which God was granting his people; and as he did so, he said, "This is the blood of the covenant." His words would later be echoed in Jesus' statement at the last supper: "This is my blood of the covenant." Since the awkwardness of the phrase reflects the original Aramaic underlying it, Paul and Luke preen the text and render it as "This cup is the new covenant in my blood."

We should add that Jesus is himself the paschal lamb of this new covenant. As we have seen, the words over the bread and over the wine are like two hands enclosing the ritual eating of the paschal lamb and thus suggesting this transposition. Without any further explanation, Paul could write, "Christ, our Passover, has been sacrificed" (1 Corinthians 5:7), so familiar must the image of the paschal lamb have become to the early community; and John (19:46), for his part, applies to the crucified Christ a text which refers directly to the paschal lamb: "Nor must you break any bone of it" (Exodus 12:46). There is no denying that this typology remains fairly discreet in the gospel text itself, but Jesus was able to develop it at length in his paschal homily.

THE SERVANT OF YAHWEH,
"COVENANT OF THE PEOPLE"

We know that the early community liked to read Jesus' own story in the prophecies about the servant of Yahweh.[3] The vocation of this just man, crushed by suffering for the sin of his brothers and then exalted and glorified by God, announces the very mystery of Jesus, "the holy servant" (Acts 4:27, 30; 3:26), humiliated in death upon the cross and then "proclaimed Son of God in all his power through his resurrection from the dead" (Romans 1:4). It also affirms the ecclesial character of his vocation: just as the servant of Yahweh is sometimes an individual. and sometimes a collective person, so Jesus' vocation concerns at one and the same time not only his own mystery but also the entire community of believers which he draws into his passion and resurrection.

This presence of the servant underlies the institution narrative:

New Testament	Isaiah
The night *he was delivered up*.	*Delivering himself up* to death (53:12).
This is my blood of the *covenant*	I have appointed you as *covenant* of the people (42:6).
poured out	He *poured out* [Hebr.] his soul in death (53:12).
for *many* for the forgiveness of *sins*.	He was bearing the *sins* of *many* (53:12).

---

[3] Isaiah 42:1-9; 49:1-6; 50:4-11; 52:13 to 53:12.

We have sometimes let ourselves be hypnotized by the consecratory value of the words to the point of forgetting their
richness on the biblical level. But this richness transfigures the
account; like sunlight on a diamond, it reflects the prophecies
concerning the servant. He who offers his body and blood for
the salvation of the world is also "a light to enlighten the
pagans," as Simeon sang (Luke 2:32 = Isaiah 42:6), and "the
covenant of the people" (Isaiah 42:6); upon him rests the Spirit
of Yahweh, and he enjoys the Father's favor as his well-beloved
Son (baptism and transfiguration: Matthew 3:17 and 17:5 =
Isaiah 42:1); he takes upon himself our infirmities and our sufferings (Matthew 8:17 = Isaiah 53:4); he is the prophet who announces the true faith to the nations (Matthew 12:18-21 =
Isaiah 42:1-4); he is the Just One, persecuted, crushed by suffering and bruised for our offenses, but, after his ordeal, exalted in
the light of God (Isaiah 53).

We should underscore the covenant theme: Jesus not only
concludes this covenant, but, as is said of the servant (Isaiah
42:6), he himself *is* this covenant. How must that be understood? We have to remember that his being, in which divinity
and humanity are bound together in the oneness of a single person, is the very source from which his mission flows. He enlight-
ens the nations because he himself is the light; he is universal
reconciliation because he unites in his body the dust of which
the human race is formed and the gold of godhead. So, too, he
seals the covenant between God and men because he is the
covenant—in other words, he unites humanity and divinity in
his person; his body is like the dwelling of love where man, now
that hostility has been killed (Ephesians 2:16), rediscovers in-
timacy with God at the same time as peace with his brothers.

THE UNIVERSAL COVENANT

According to the Matthew-Mark tradition, the blood of the
covenant was poured out "for many." Quite a few translations
read "for the multitude"—which gives a far better text. In point

of fact, the original Greek has "for many" and reflects the Aramaic which Jesus spoke. Now, in Aramaic (and in Hebrew), the word *many* may have an exclusive sense as in English ("many"—therefore, "not all") or an inclusive sense ("really many"—that is, "all"). This Semitism explains many passages which could otherwise be problematic. Thus Jesus states that "many sins"—that is to say, "all her sins"—were forgiven the sinful woman because she loved much (Luke 7:47).[4] Similarly, Paul explains that "as by one man's [Adam's] disobedience, many [that is, 'all'] were made sinners, so by one man's [Christ's] obedience, many [that is, 'all'] will be made righteous" (Romans 5:19). In the account of the institution, we must understand that the blood poured out "for many" was in reality poured out "for all men." Jesus' last meal with his followers was also the first truly universal meal, the first ecumenical passover, where the whole human family was invited and mystically gathered together.

The universality of the covenant does not gainsay the particular election of Israel or the preferential love God bears it. Quite the contrary, it is rooted in them. The election of Israel is a service of the nations, Jewish particularism is a door of hope for all the peoples of the earth: Israel is the royal and priestly people, born of the covenant on Sinai (Exodus 19:6), whom God has placed between himself and the nations. But the newness of the covenant at the last supper resides in the quality of the mediator (cf. Hebrews 8:6-13). The brotherhood of all men invited to God's one table is no longer founded on unity of race (as for Israel) or similarity of calling (as for the nations), but on the fact that the whole of humanity has been adopted in Jesus Christ and that each man truly becomes a son of God in the only Son.

What role did the Twelve play at this banquet of the new covenant? They represented the twelve tribes of Israel which, according to tradition (Exodus 24:4), had assisted at the cove-

---

[4]Among the more recent translations, *The Jerusalem Bible*, *The New American Bible* and *The New English Bible* solve the difficulty by speaking of "her many sins" being forgiven.—Translator.

nant on Sinai. They also prefigured the Church of the New Testament, that new Jerusalem built "on twelve foundation stones, each one of which [bears] the name of one of the twelve apostles of the Lamb" (Revelation 21:14). In them, the Church received the Eucharistized bread and wine for the first time and handed this memorial down to future ages.

III

The Eucharist as Thanksgiving

THE WORD *EUCHARIST*

The word *eucharist* is the Anglicization of a Greek word meaning "thanksgiving." *Eucharistein* is to say "thank you." In a votive offering (from perhaps the second century) to the healer-god Aesculapius, a soldier tells his story as follows: "He recovered his sight, he came back, he thanked—*eucharistesen*—the god publicly."

That is the sense in which the Greek Bible uses the verb *eucharistein*. Judith, for instance, harangues her fellow citizens of Bethulia in these words: "Let us give thanks *[eucharistesomen]* to the Lord our God who, as he tested our ancestors, is now testing us" (Judith 8:25). The Samaritan leper "eucharists" Jesus, who healed him (Luke 17:16). The Pharisee, for his part, "eucharists" God because he is not like the rest of men (Luke 18:11). And at Lazarus' tomb, Jesus "eucharists" his Father for always hearing him (John 11:41).

The texts most closely related to the last supper are doubt-lessly those concerning the multiplication of the loaves, which the synoptics place in what is called "the bread section" (Mark 6:35 to 8:26). In the first miracle, Mark 8:6, followed by Mat-thew 15:36, proposes a quasi-liturgical text: "He took the seven loaves, and after giving thanks *[eucharistesen]*, he broke them and handed them to his disciples."

The account of the first multiplication indubitably reports the same miracle, but in a different recension. Here, Mark 6:41, Matthew 14:18 and Luke 9:16 use the verb *eulogein*, meaning "to say the blessing," while the parallel passage in John 6:11 carries *eucharistein*. In the Old Testament, *eulogy* corresponds rather to "blessing" *(berakhah)*, whereas *eucharist* corresponds to "thanksgiving" *(todah)*.[1] For the early Christian community, however, the two terms were practically synonymous. Explain-ing why the charismatic groups in Corinth should pray "not only with the spirit but with the mind as well"—that is, in such a way as to be understood—Paul tells them: "Any uninitiated person will never be able to say Amen to your thanksgiving ["eucharist"], if you only bless ["eulogize"] God with the spirit, for he will have no idea what you are saying. However well you make your thanksgiving ["eucharist"], the other gets no benefit from it" (1 Corinthians 14:16-17).

In the narrative of the last supper, the Matthew-Mark tra-dition uses the verb *eulogize* for the bread and the verb *eucharistize* for the wine, whereas the Antiochian Paul-Luke tradition uses only *eucharistize*. Yet both cases deal with the blessing as well as the thanksgiving Jesus addressed to his Fa-ther on taking the bread and the wine.

By a convenient ellipsis, the name *thanksgiving* was eventu-ally applied to the bread and the wine over which the prayer had been recited. In the beginning—say, during the 50's—in Corinth, either term, *eucharist* or *eulogy*, could have won out, and our Eucharist today could very well have been called

---

[1]The *todah* is a category of *shelamin* sacrifice (see p. 72). This sacrificial and "eucharistic" meal comprises a proclamation of God's greatness. See H. Cazel-les, "L'anaphore et l'Ancien Testament," in *Eucharisties d'Orient et d'Occident* (Paris: Cerf, "Lex Orandi," 46), pp. 11-21.

eulogy; but in the flux of history, it was *eucharist* which finally triumphed. Toward the middle of the second century, Justin bore witness to this evolution (see p. 26), and in three statements his text clearly sums up the linguistic growth and the life of this word:

> The one who is presiding . . . makes a long *eucharist* [that is, a prayer of thanksgiving] . . .
> Those whom we call deacons distribute the consecrated bread [that is, bread over which the prayer has been said— "*eucharistized* bread," writes Justin, as Paul writes of the "eulogized cup"] . . .
> We call this food "Eucharist."

There, in a few broad strokes, is the evolution of the word *eucharist*. I now wish to show—and this is what matters most— how our Eucharist is thanksgiving.

THANKSGIVING IN JEWISH PIETY

"To do this" in memory of Christ is, above all, to offer up his thanksgiving anew. Of course, this is not a matter of repeating his words verbatim in loving mime, but, far more truly and profoundly, of cultivating a spiritual attitude which relives his praise and thanksgiving. Actually, even though he stamped it with his personality, there was nothing exceptional about his blessing over the bread and the wine. Quite the opposite: it fit into Israel's daily prayer patterns and, most especially, echoed the innumerable blessings which characterized Jewish piety and transfigured a believer's life into a continuous eucharistic feast.

Blessing is a basic attitude in Yahwism. The epiphany of God's love, which flashes forth in creation and human history, is answered by man's thanks and praise. Yahweh speaks by fashioning marvels, and man replies by blessing the God of those marvels. When God's love floods over Israel's life—and well did they know that all his ways are love (Psalm 25:10)— what can believers do but joyfully welcome this tenderness pouring down from heaven, then bless and give thanks?

Everyone is familiar with the delightful episode in which the Yahwistic tradition has garnered a family's recollections of Isaac's marriage. At Abraham's bidding, his eldest servant took ten camels and set out for Upper Mesopotamia and the town of Nahor to find Isaac a wife who would share not only the tribe's blood but its same faith. By Nahor's well, at the hour when evening sings in the sky, God showed him the beautiful Rebekah. "Then the man bowed down and worshipped Yahweh saying 'Blessed be Yahweh, God of my master Abraham, for he has not stopped showing kindness and goodness to my master. Yahweh has guided my steps to the house of my master's brother' " (Genesis 24:26-27).

Here, blessing is externalized in an adoring obeisance; it feeds on admiration for God; and, lastly, it makes commemoration ("anamnesis," as the liturgy says) of the divine wonders: Yahweh has lavished his kindness on Abraham and guided his servant's steps. We have here the essential structure of "Eucharistic" prayer as found in the Bible and in the liturgy: thanksgiving and anamnesis of God's wonders.

It is only natural that piety should have hewn such blessings into set formulas and that tradition, always in search of beauty, should have woven them a vestment of splendor. Not every evening was a Rebekah to be found at Nahor's well, but every day the wondrous God was to be extolled amid the routine banality. Because earth is an immense temple where creation shouts "Glory!" (Psalm 29:9), because every period of its life is in God's hands (Psalm 31:16), the whole of Jewish existence is a face-to-face conversation with the Eternal, every encounter with creatures creates praise and becomes eucharist. On waking in the morning and seeing the sunlight, on rising, on washing and dressing, eating and drinking, inhaling a pleasant fragrance, meeting a friend or receiving good news—in a word, on every occasion, the soul of Israel hears itself in the psalmist's cry:

Blessed be Yahweh, who performs
marvels of love for me! (Psalm 31:21.)

In this connection, it is appropriate to quote the *Shemone Esre* or *Eighteen [Blessings]*—so much the most representative prayer of Judaism that it is also called *Tephillah*: "the Prayer" *par excellence*. The eighteen blessings contained in it form the warp and woof of a long prayer of praise and petition to be recited three times a day. Its essential elements date back to the pre-Christian era. Here is the opening stanza, with later additions enclosed in brackets:

> Blessed be you, O Yahweh,
> [our God and God of our fathers],
> God of Abraham, of Isaac and Jacob,
> [great God, redoubtable and mighty],
> most high God, creator of heaven and earth,
> our shield and the shield of our fathers,
> [our confidence in every generation].
> Blessed be you, O Yahweh, shield of Abraham!

Eighteen times, like a luminous refrain amid a chant of supplication, there bursts forth the cry "Blessed be you, O Yahweh!" The soul of Israel reveals itself here, unable to ask anything without giving thanks, unwilling to extend its hand to beg without first raising it to bless.

Jesus always expressed his piety with a certain reserve, as if not to disclose the plenitude of love which bound him to the Father. (Only once—in John 14:31—does he say he loves the Father.) However, he allows his "Eucharistic" soul to show through in the blessing which is known as the "Hymn of Jubilation" and which takes its opening words precisely from the *Shemone Esre*. "Filled with joy by the Holy Spirit," as Luke reports (10:21-22), he said:

> I bless you, Father,
> Lord of heaven and of earth,
> for hiding these things from the learned and the clever
> and revealing them to mere children.
> Yes, Father, for that is what it pleased you to do.

Without a doubt we have here the highest expression of Jesus' religion—a religion compounded of admiration, blessing and praise for the loving will of the Father. This "Yes, Father," spoken here in the jubilation of the Holy Spirit, would sound again in the humble prayer in Gethsemane: "Abba (Father)! Everything is possible for you" (Mark 14:36).

Jesus' prayer at the last supper is not the thanksgiving of an instant. It is the reflection of a life which was entirely "Eucharistic."

PASCHAL THANKSGIVING

Can we spell out the themes of that praise at the last supper? Yes, for the last supper was situated in the context of the passover, and Jesus' praise accordingly took up the themes of the paschal feast. Now, as we saw in the *Poem of the Four Nights* (see p. 35), this celebration commemorated the night God created the world, the night Abraham offered up his son Isaac, the night God freed his people from bondage in Egypt, and the night at the end of time which he will open to an eternal dawn.

The passover and creation

To celebrate the passover was, first of all, to give thanks for the marvels of creation. That is precisely what the Great Hallel does (Psalm 136). Jesus sang it with his apostles at the last supper (Matthew 26:30 and Mark 14:26 mention it explicitly); in one same burst of praise, he proclaimed the love of God that invented the universe and liberated the exodus people, the love that established the earth upon the waters and gave the promised land as an inheritance. For the Israelites, creation prefaced "redemption"; they praised God as readily for counting the stars and feeding the ravens as for building Jerusalem and gathering up its deportees (Psalm 147); they never forgot that the Book of Exodus is introduced by Genesis.

This link between the passover and creation was further underlined by the scriptural readings used in the liturgy of the synagogue. In Palestine, the cycle of readings ran three years. Now, the first year began in the paschal month of Nisan precisely with the account of creation in Genesis 1; and the second began with Exodus 12:2, which declares, "This month will be for you the first month of the year." The liturgy, therefore, wove an affective bond between the feast of creation and that of the exodus. The passover, a time of vernal joy, also became a memorial of creation. In the words of an ancient paschal homily, it was "the flowering of creation, the beauty of the world."[2] It was also the feast of light—of the "eternal day," as they liked to put it—since, at the spring equinox, the sun shines twelve hours over the day and the full moon twelve hours over the night.

All these themes, naturally, have been "Christianized" in the passover of Christ, transfigured by the glory of the risen Lord. "To do this" in his memory is to follow his example and praise the Creator for the seas and the mountains he holds in the hollow of his hand, but especially for the new heavens and the new earth inaugurated by the resurrection; to bless the Father for fashioning the first man from the clay of the earth, but especially for forming the new Adam, whose resurrection flows back over the world in a ceaseless wave of life and joy (cf. Romans 5:12-21). Christians sing the "eternal light" of the spring equinox, but especially the Sun of life and immortality who shines in their hearts (cf. 2 Timothy 1:10); they thank God for the springtime that mantles the hillsides in flowers and germinates the first fruits of the harvest for the passover, but especially for the unending springtime which the door of eternity now opens to them. Though they see that sin has flawed the harmony of creation and faded its beauty like a rose scattered on the autumn wind, they know the risen Lord restores everything —the universe of heaven and of earth—in himself (cf. Ephesians 1:10, 22-23; 1 Corinthians 15:27; Revelation 21:6). Though they hear captive creation groaning under the yoke of sin and vanity (cf. Romans 8:19-22), they know these are no longer the throes of agony but the pangs of new life coming to birth. They know

---

[2]*Homélies pascales*, I: *Une homélie inspirée du Traité sur la Pâque d'Hippolyte* (Paris: Cerf, "Sources chrétiennes," 27), p. 145.

they are walking toward a new land, toward new heavens, toward a new Jerusalem as beautiful as a bride (cf. Revelation 21:1-5). In a word, as the Jewish passover was the feast of creation and springtime, so Christ's passover is the feast of the new creation and eternal springtime, with the Eucharist commemorating and rendering thanks for both.

Rightly, then, does the Roman liturgy associate creation—though timidly, one must admit—with its Eucharistic praise. "Father, you are holy indeed, and all creation rightly gives you praise," states Eucharistic Prayer III. And in Eucharistic Prayer IV, we evoke the day when, "freed from the corruption of sin and death, we shall with every creature" sing the glory of the Father.

We may wonder whether this cosmic praise flows directly from the sheer fact of the incarnation and, therefore, has no necessary connection with the Eucharist. In actuality, the transformation of this human clay into "Eucharist," the transition from carnal man to son of God, began when Jesus assumed our human nature. His divine person is situated at the summit of the human pyramid, at the terminus of its evolution. It took so long for the clay to yield a human body capable of intelligence, to germinate a human heart capable of divinity. But in Jesus, the evolution of mankind touches upon the shores of divinity; in him, through the Holy Spirit, the groping of the ages attains the only Son of the Father.

Now, Jesus is the firstborn: all his brothers follow him. Through his incarnation in the Virgin Mary, the ferment of his divinity has been placed in the heart of the earth, so that all humanity becomes in a way the body of Christ, all humanity becomes the temple which the Spirit fills with his glory, all humanity hears the Father say, "You are my son, today I have become your father" (Psalm 2:7). Having become sons in the Son, we participate in his mystery, we become "Eucharist" in the very measure we identify ourselves with him, in the measure his passover seizes us and makes us living "praise of glory" (cf. Ephesians 1:6, 12). Clement of Alexandria (d. about 215) rapturously describes the Son's Eucharistic chant within redeemed humanity: "Setting aside lyre and cithara as soulless instruments, the Word of God, through the Holy Spirit, has attuned to himself this world and especially man, who epitomizes it, together with his body and soul. With this thousand-voiced instrument, he sings of God and accompanies himself on this cithara which is man."[3]

But this process of divinization, this transformation of clay into a hymn of thanksgiving, is signified with particular intensity by the Eucharist. The grain of wheat, placed in the heart of the earth, germinated under the kiss of the springtime sun, and crowned with golden heads ripe for harvesting and baking into bread for man, is here changed into the body of the Son of God! And the blood of the grape, bronzed in autumn sunshine, is changed into the blood of the risen Christ! Creation becomes Eucharist, bread and wine become praise of glory, the fruit of man's work becomes Christ. It is no longer just a sign of God (demonstrating his existence as does everything that comes from his hands), and no longer just a bearer of his grace (as in the other sacraments). Transubstantiated, it is eternal life, the body of the Son of God.

Thus, the Eucharist reveals the ultimate meaning of God's creative act: the vocation of the entire universe. This supreme significance does not consist in the fact of coming from God, of being created from nothing *(ex nihilo)*—as if God, after holding the earth in his hands were plunging it into the blind round dance of the ages, into the nullity of the cosmic world which turns in circles without ever moving ahead. Rather, it consists in a progression of matter toward man, of man toward Christ, and of Christ toward the Father. This return of the creature Godward, this metamorphosis of slaves' groaning (cf. Romans 8:22) into a filial hymn of praise, is signified by the Eucharist in a way which transcends all the other sacraments. The moment of consecration—when the bread and the wine, "fruit of the earth and work of human hands," become the body of Christ—consummates in the twinkling of an eye the march of the centuries toward God. Predestined by the Father, called to existence in the Son, "the first-born of all creation" (Colossians 1:15), and

---

[3]*Protrepticus*, I, 5.

led by the Spirit, who moves all the children of God (cf.
Romans 8:4), man—and the creation he sums up in himself—
returns "to the Father's heart" (John 1:18), that heart where the
Son is found and the love of the Spirit reigns. There, in the immutable peace of God, is the end toward which every movement
of grace is directed, and most especially the sending of the Son
among mankind and the gift of his Spirit. Born in the heart of
God and transubstantiated in the Eucharist, creation returns
into the heart of God, there eternally to "praise the glory of his
grace" (Ephesians 1:6).

The passover and Abraham's sacrifice

The second night commemorated at the Jewish passover
was that of Abraham's sacrifice.

The unique place Abraham occupies in Israel's history is
well known. He was father to "the people of the promise" not
only in the flesh but even more in faith. Now, that faith cul-
minated in his sacrifice of Isaac. With almost litanic tenderness,
God had demanded this supreme sacrifice from the patriarch:
"Take your son, your only child Isaac, whom you love, and go
to the land of Moriah. There you shall offer him as a burnt offering, on a mountain I will point out to you" (Genesis 22:2).
And Abraham had obeyed. Paul, in his letter to the Hebrews,
comments: "It was by faith that Abraham, when put to the test,
offered up Isaac. He offered to sacrifice his only son even
though the promises had been made to him. . . . He was confident that God had the power even to raise the dead" (Hebrews
11:17, 19).

Now, Jewish tradition placed the sacrificing of Isaac in
direct relation with the passover. The *Book of Jubilees*, an apo-
cryphal work from the second century before Christ, affirms
that Isaac was offered up on the fourteenth of Nisan at the very
hour the paschal lamb would later be immolated; that the
mountain of holocaust was none other than Mount Sion (2
Chronicles 3:1 had already identified Mount Moriah—the
mountain of the sacrifice, in Genesis—with the hill where the

Temple would later rise); and that just as Isaac, the firstborn, was redeemed by the blood of a ram, so all the firstborn of the Hebrews would be saved by the blood of the paschal lamb.

According to tradition also, Isaac agreed to his immolation in a spirit of total oblativity and divine peace, and this sacrifice afforded Abraham an opportunity to intercede for all his descendants.

Let us here quote the targum on Genesis 22, surely one of the most moving texts in all Jewish literature:

> Abraham said to Isaac, "A lamb will be prepared for holocaust in the sight of Yahweh. Otherwise, you will be the lamb for the holocaust." And they walked on together, with stout hearts.
>
> They reached the mountain Yahweh had spoken of, and Abraham built the altar there. He piled the wood, bound his son Isaac, and placed him over it upon the altar. Then he reached out and took the knife to sacrifice his son Isaac.
>
> Isaac spoke and said to Abraham his father, "Father mine, bind me fast lest I resist you." [. . .] Abraham's eyes were fixed on Isaac's, and Isaac's were turned toward the angels from above. But Abraham did not see them. At that moment there came a voice from heaven saying, "Come and see the two 'unique ones' in my universe. One sacrifices, and the other is sacrificed. The one who sacrifices does not hesitate, and the one who is sacrificed stretches forth his throat." [. . .]
>
> Abraham began to pray and invoked the name of the Word of Yahweh, saying, "I beg you, by your mercy, Yahweh! [. . .] There has been no division in my heart from the moment you told me to sacrifice my son Isaac and reduce him to dust and ashes before you. Instead, I rose immediately, early in the morning, and hurried to carry out your words with joy. I have executed your commandment. Therefore, when his children are in distress, remember the sacrifice of their father Isaac and hear the voice of their entreaty. Answer and deliver them from all tribulation!"[4]

That was what Jesus was celebrating; that was the subject of his paschal thanksgiving. "To do this" in memory of him is

---

[4]See *Neophyti I*, Vol. 1: *Genesis* (Madrid-Barcelona, 1968), pp. 405-406.

to render thanks for the faith of Abraham, who built the people of the covenant, for his obedient love in sacrificing his son, for Isaac's heroic acceptance of God's will over him, and for the intercessory prayer in behalf of their descendants when trials should come.

These themes, like those of creation, are "accomplished"—that is, brought to their fullness—in the new covenant. For, in Jesus, the Father is "mindful of his mercy—according to the promise he made to our ancestors—of his mercy to Abraham and to his descendants for ever," as that daughter of Abraham, the Virgin Mary, declared (Luke 1:54-55). In Jesus, all the promises find their "yes" (2 Corinthians 1:20). In him, the promised land is no longer the region of Canaan, but the heaven of the risen Lord. In him, posterity, innumerable as the sand on the seashore or the stars in the sky, is formed no longer by the tribes of Israel, but by the universal family of all God's children through faith. In him, the son of Abraham becomes Son of God. Such is the motive of Christian paschal praise.

Abraham and Isaac prefigure the fullness of God's love for the world:

—Abraham, who "did not spare his beloved son" (cf. Genesis 22:12, Greek), foreshadows the Father, who "did not spare his own Son" (Romans 8:32) but "loved the world so much that he gave his only Son" (John 3:16).

—Isaac, on the holocaustal pyre, his smiling eyes turned heavenward in ready acceptance of death, foreshadows Christ, who loved us and gave himself up in our place "as a fragrant offering and a sacrifice to God" (Ephesians 5:2). In his passover homily at the last supper, Jesus commented on his own death: "A man can have no greater love than to lay down his life for his friends" (John 15:13).

Neither Isaac's blood nor the slaughter of a ram constituted the sacrifice, but rather the attitude of the aged patriarch and his only son. And it was valid only insofar as it was the expression of love. Isaac being reborn, as it were, from the ashes of his holocaust, and Jesus rising in the splendor of the resurrection, are God's answer to man's sacrifice.

Fittingly, then, does the Roman liturgy, in the memorial

prayer after the consecration (Eucharistic Prayer I), recall
Abraham: "Look with favor on these offerings and accept them
as once you accepted . . . the sacrifice of Abraham, our father
in faith."

The passover and the exodus

The third night which the Jewish passover commemorated
was that of the exodus.

Yahwism was a historical religion, and the exodus was the
heart of that history. And since history is always more beautiful
when contemplated from a distance that permits the healing of
the wounds sustained along the way, Israel invested the exodus
with all the tenderness that had eased its adolescence. The mi-
gration of the sheepherding tribes in search of waterholes became the triumphal procession of a whole nation of priests and
kings in their march toward the promised land. It was amid the
crags of Sinai that God set a table for his people and fed them
"on pure wheat and . . . with the wild rock honey" (Psalm
81:16); the exquisite sweetness of this angelic bread, which
adapted itself to each one's taste, manifested the Father's
kindness toward his children (Wisdom 16:20-21). Scorning the
fetid water from the cisterns in the desert, God delighted in
causing a new source of living water to spring forth from the
rock which—according to a targumic tradition alluded to in 1
Corinthians 10:4—"followed them as they went." There, in the
desert of Sinai, Yahweh revealed his name—not the In-
comprehensible of the burning bush, but the one whom every
child of Israel, from the least to the greatest, could grasp and
interpret: "Yahweh, Yahweh, a God of tenderness and compassion, slow to anger, rich in kindness and faithfulness" (Exodus
34:6). There, too, he proclaimed his law, entrusting to his beloved, not a set of regulations or some anonymous code of
taboos, but instead "the Ten Words of the Covenant" (Exodus
34:28), which Israel in turn received, not with a sigh as if they
were a burden, but with praise and thanksgiving, for the law is
joy for the heart, light for the eyes, comfort for the soul, wis-

dom for the simple, and always sweeter than honey (cf. Psalm 19:8-10). And there, lastly, in the dazzling solitude of the steppes, he adopted Israel as his firstborn son, from the midst of all the other nations (Deuteronomy 32), and gave it—like his own heart—his most precious gift: the covenant. Yahweh became the God of Israel, and Israel became the people of God.

Such was the exodus for which Jesus gave thanks. For the Jews celebrated, not the anniversary of an age-old story which they read about in a family album called "the Bible," but a mystery which they actualized every spring. "In each generation," states the *Mishnah*, "each man ought to consider himself as having personally come out of Egypt. For it is written (Exodus 13:8): 'On that day you will explain to your son, "This is because of what Yahweh did for me when I came out of Egypt" ' " (*Pesahim*, X, 5). This actualization was signified somewhat theatrically by the fact that the celebrants mimed the passover, so to speak: they would eat the lamb hastily (Deuteronomy 16:1-8), with a girdle round their waist, sandals on their feet and a staff in their hand, as if they had to flee from some invisible pharaoh (Exodus 12:11), and they used unleavened bread, "the bread of emergency" (Deuteronomy 16:3), which had not had time to rise, so hurried had been the departure. Even though these ritual prescriptions were not all observed in Jesus' day, the essential remained: each passover celebration relived the exodus and, by eliciting thanks, realized the prophecy, "The people I have formed for myself will sing my praises" (Isaiah 43:21).

These exodist themes form the heart of Israel's religion. Venerable though they be, they are nevertheless transcended in the framework of the new covenant. Or, rather, Jesus' death and resurrection—his "exodus," as Luke calls it (9:31)—transfigure them into a Christian passover. For what the exodus means to Israel, the death of Jesus means to Christians: going from this vale of tears, passing "from this world to the Father" (John 13:1), entering into the glory of the resurrection. In this Christian passover, Jesus himself is the sacrificial lamb (Exodus 12:46 = John 19:36). "Christ, our passover, has been sacrificed," Paul writes quite simply (1 Corinthians 5:7), as if this theme were universally known by the faithful who, he explains, form a "completely new batch of bread, unleavened," for this messianic feast. Pilgrims of the Christian exodus, they must "free [their] minds of encumbrances" (1 Peter 1:13) and be "scrupulously careful" during this exile (v. 17), for they have been redeemed "in the precious blood of a lamb without spot or stain, namely Christ" (v. 19).

To Israel's thanksgiving for the Jewish passover, Christians add thanksgiving for Jesus' passover, for his death, his resurrection and his ascension (cf. the anamnesis). They offer thanks for deliverance from the prison Egypt was, but even more for the well-beloved Son's entrance into the glory of the Father. They offer thanks for the crossing of the Red Sea, which was like a baptism "in this cloud and in this sea" (1 Corinthians 10:2), but even more for their own baptism, which delivered them from death and sin, and led them to the shores of the land of eternal freedom in the risen Lord. They offer thanks for the pillar of fire that illuminated the darkness of the desert, but even more for the true light which is Christ, who rises over the darkness of the heart and guides the strays toward life (John 8:12). They offer thanks for the manna in the desert, but even more for the bread of God which gives life to the world (John 6:33): the feast in the desert merely foreshadowed "the wedding feast of the Lamb" (Revelation 19:9). They offer thanks for Moses, "the faithful servant" (Hebrews 3:5) and guide of the redeemed community, but even more for Jesus, the new Moses whom the Father established, because of his sonship, "as the master in the house; and we are his house" (Hebrews 3:6). They offer thanks for the springs of living water God unsealed in the steppes, but even more for "the spring welling up to eternal life" (John 4:14) dug for them by faith in Jesus: "The Lamb . . . will be their shepherd and will lead them to springs of living water" (Revelation 7:17). They offer thanks for the law promulgated—according to tradition—fifty days after the departure from Egypt, but even more for the Spirit of Jesus, the new law diffused in their hearts in waves of love (Romans 5:5) on the feast of Pentecost, fifty days after his resurrection. They offer thanks for the covenant concluded on Sinai, but even more for the new covenant in

Christ's blood: "Though the Law was given through Moses, grace and truth have come through Jesus Christ" (John 1:17). They sing the canticle of Moses, but this canticle is also that of the Lamb (Revelation 15:3), who is worshiped in the heavenly liturgy of the Book of Revelation (15:2-4). In short, the Jewish pasch celebrates the exodus of Israel. The Christian pasch celebrates the exodus of Jesus. The Eucharist commemorates both at one and the same time.

With good reason, therefore, the Church recalls Jesus' death and resurrection at the very heart of the Eucharistic celebration. She does so, first, at the beginning of the institution narrative, in keeping with the Pauline tradition (1 Corinthians 11:23); and then again, after the consecration, in the double anamnesis proclaimed by the assembly and then taken up by the priest. No doubt, the most explicit example is Eucharistic Prayer IV:

> Father, we now celebrate this memorial of our redemption.
> We recall Christ's death, his descent among the dead,
> his resurrection, and his ascension to your right hand. . . .
> We offer you his body and blood.

The Mass is the celebrating of Jesus' passover. It is linked to the last supper, where the consecration of the bread and the consecration of the wine after the meal were like two hands surrounding the sacrificial meal of the paschal lamb. Thus, the last supper is rooted in the passover of Israel and in that of Jesus; and the Christian Eucharist actualizes both at the same time.

The passover and the eternal feast

The fourth night commemorated at the passover was that of the end of time, "when the world comes to an end in order to be redeemed . . . and the Messiah King will descend from on high" (cf. p. 35). The exodus, a celebration of the past, is also a feast of hope, for each passover prefigures that eschatological and messianic day. "On that night, they were saved," people used to repeat; "on this night, they will be saved." At midnight, the Temple gates were thrown open, as if to hasten and welcome the triumphal entry of Yahweh or his messenger. For the prophecy announced, "The Lord you are seeking will suddenly enter his Temple; and the angel of the covenant whom you are longing for, yes, he is coming!" (Malachi 3:1).

It is in this messianic fervor that the prayers of the Hallel were recited. The blessing which accompanied them read thus: "O Lord our God and the God of our fathers, bring us in peace to the other set feasts and festivals which are coming to meet us, while we rejoice in the building-up of the city and are joyful in thy worship; and may we eat there of the sacrifices and of the Passover-offerings whose blood has reached with acceptance the wall of thy Altar . . . Blessed are thou, O Lord, who has redeemed Israel!"[5] Particularly significant is the interpretation of Psalm 118, which closes the Hallel (Psalms 113-118). Verse 24 —"This is the day made memorable by Yahweh"—was applied, as well it might be, to that eschatological day which God, at the end of time, would fill with gladness. The midrash on this psalm pictures a grandiose procession leading the messianic king into the Holy City as the inhabitants on the ramparts and the pilgrims from Judah dialogue in the psalmist's words:

> From inside, the men of Jerusalem will say,
>   "Blessed be he that cometh IN the name of the Lord!" (v. 26a).
> And from outside, the men of Judah will say,
>   "We bless you OUT of the house of the Lord!" (v. 26b).
> From inside, the men of Jerusalem will say,
>   "The Lord is God and hath given us light" (v. 27a).
> And from outside, the men of Judah will say,
>   "Order the festival procession with boughs, even unto the horns of the altar!" (v. 27b).
> From inside, the men of Jerusalem will say,
>   "Thou art my God, and I will give thanks unto Thee!" (v. 28a).
> And from outside, the men of Judah will say,
>   "Thou art my God, I will exalt Thee!" (v. 28b).
> Then the men of Jerusalem and the men of Judah, together,
> opening their mouths in praise of the Holy One, blessed be He, will say:

---

[5]*Pesahim, X, 6.* H. Damby, *The Mishnah* (Oxford University Press, 1933), p. 151.

"O give thanks unto the Lord, for He is good, for His mercy
endureth for ever" (v. 29).[6]

In Jewish tradition, then, the praise of the paschal Hallel concludes with a unanimous acclamation. With one heart and one voice, pilgrims and inhabitants of Jerusalem extol God's eternal love. "The day made memorable by Yahweh" is the day of "him who comes in the name of Yahweh." It will mark the beginning, for all eternity, of a Eucharistic feast which will never end.

The evangelists contrived, in their accounts, to afford us the joy of discovering traces of these eschatological expectations. For instance, when Jesus, a pilgrim in Jerusalem in messianic times, entered the Holy City to celebrate the true passover, "the crowds" (Matthew 21:9), waving the branches mentioned in Psalm 118:27, ran to meet him with shouts of joy, and the acclamations which rose to their lips came directly from the Hallel:

Hosanna to the Son of David!
Blessings on him who comes in the name of the Lord![7]

It is noticeable, too, how the eschatological parables have Jesus returning during the night. "But at midnight there was a cry, 'The bridegroom is here! Go out and meet him' " (Matthew 25:6). Accordingly, the ten bridesmaids—ten is exactly the number of guests required for the passover—must keep the lamp of vigilance burning. It is necessary to keep watch all night, therefore, so as to appear "standing" before the Son of Man (Luke 21:36). Happy those servants who, obeying the paschal rubric, remain "dressed for action" (Luke 12:35) in order to greet their master when he returns in the dead of night.

---

[6]In J. Jeremias, *The Eucharistic Words of Jesus*, pp. 257-258.

[7]Psalm 118:25-26; Matthew 21:9; Mark 11:9; Luke 19:38; John 12:13. *Hosanna* comes from the Hebrew *hoshi ah na* (Psalm 118:25), meaning "Oh, grant salvation!"

Of all Jewish feasts, the passover was the richest in eschatological and messianic hope. The account of the last supper
bears faithful testimony to that wealth. There, Jesus declares
that he will not eat the passover again "until it is fulfilled in the
kingdom of God" or drink any more wine "until the kingdom
of God comes" (Luke 22:16 and 18). The formulation is akin to
vows of desistance. Thus, according to Psalm 132:2-5, David
pledged to sleep no more until he had found a resting-place for
the ark of the covenant—which clearly meant he was binding
himself primarily to locating a home for the ark and secondarily, as a sign of this endeavor, refraining from even closing his
eyelids until he had succeeded. Likewise, in Acts 23:12-13, the
Judaizers "made a vow not to eat or drink until they had killed
Paul"—which, again, meant that their principal purpose was to
murder him. So, too, in the *logia* (words) from the last supper,
we have a principal affirmation and, secondarily, an affirmation
of desistance.

In the secondary affirmation, Jesus engages himself to celebrate no further passovers. This one is truly the last; and, with
this formula of desistance, he precludes all possibility of coming
back on his word. Practically speaking, such a decision was tan-
tamount to prophesying his death. Since the day of his transfiguration, when Moses and Elijah had already spoken of his
"exodus" to Jerusalem, his life had been magnetized, so to
speak, by that woeful/triumphant departure from this world.[8]
His cross, a gibbet for criminals, would be a throne of glory and
exaltation (John 12:32), and the tomb which was to imprison his
corpse in stone would become a door for angels, open to the ascension. In a prophetic gesture, Mary, the woman with the ala-
baster vase, had already anointed his body as if for burial
(Mark 14:8). On this very day began the first of those three
days after which he would attain to his perfection (Luke 13:32).

---

[8]See the announcements of the passion: the first, in Matthew 16:21-23; Mark
8:31-33 and Luke 9:22; the second, in Matthew 17:22-23; Mark 9:30-32 and
Luke 9:43-45; and the third, in Matthew 20:17-19; Mark 10:32-34 and Luke
18:31-34. Though their redaction was perhaps influenced by the account of the
passion, these announcements nevertheless reveal that Jesus understood he had
to undergo the "passion" of the servant of Yahweh (cf. Isaiah 52:13 to 53:12).

This hour of anguish and glory is illumined with an immense hope. For the principal affirmation bears squarely on the fact that the passover will one day be "fulfilled"—in other words, brought to its perfection in the kingdom. For centuries Israel had been heaping up the years on the threshing floor of history, and the passovers had accumulated indefinitely without ever surpassing themselves. Now, on the horizon of time, there loomed a passover that was finally perfect: a fullness of joy and festivity, of praise and thanksgiving, an infinite liberation in a new creation built according to God's eternal love. Therefore, Jesus' desistance—he will no longer celebrate the passover—will last only for a while, the years allotted to the history of the world. Once that span of time has passed—the blinking of an eye, compared to eternity!—Jesus will again drink the festive wine in his Father's kingdom. Then, on that day created for eternity, will begin the "fulfilled" passover, the eschatological feast which will mark the inauguration of the new world: "Yahweh Sabaoth will prepare for all peoples a banquet of rich food, a banquet of fine wines. . . . He will destroy Death for ever. The Lord Yahweh will wipe away the tears from every cheek" (Isaiah 25:6-8).

Finally, let us note the humility of the words "I shall not drink wine until the day I drink the new wine with you in the kingdom of my Father" (Matthew 26:29). Jesus is not the organizer of this eternal passover: the Father will be the master of the feast, in "his" kingdom. Jesus himself, as Son—and this is perhaps the humblest statement he ever made in praise of his Father—even accepts nescience of the appointed day and hour (Mark 13:32). At the passover of the last supper, as at each Eucharist, he provides the wine for the feast, his own blood; but, at the feast of the fulfilled passover, he will take his place among the guests: "I will drink it with you," he tells his disciples.[9]

It is easy to imagine with what fervent love the early Christians strained toward the day of that eternal feast with Jesus.

[9] See the parable in Luke 12:35-37, where Jesus states that the master "will put on an apron, sit them down at table and wait on them" (v. 37) if he finds them vigilant—a mere parabolic detail, perhaps, but meaningful.

They had drunk the wine of his last passover with him; and now that he had left them for the glory of heaven, they found themselves immersed once again in the hard reality of every day, torn and anguished in their loneliness, or, more simply, wearied and depressed by an existence far from the face of the Lord. Therefore, it was normal that each Eucharist should intensify their expectation of the day when the number of guests for the feast would finally be complete and the sacramental signs, henceforth unnecessary, would be replaced by his corporal presence as on the night of the last passover. Thus, the Eucharistized bread and wine, signs of Christ "until he comes" (1 Corinthians 11:26), are at the same time prayers for the day of his advent. They proclaim his presence under the sacramental signs, they reveal his absence at the level of sense perception, and they implore his coming for the day of eternity.

The liturgy felicitously highlights the last supper's eschatological dimension. In the anamnesis after the consecration, it recalls the early Christians' *"Marana tha*: Come, Lord" (1 Corinthians 16:22) and begs, "Lord Jesus, come in glory!" Each Mass is a door of hope opened upon eternity.

This mystery is realized with particular intensity in communion received as viaticum. As is well known, this practice dates back to Christian antiquity: even in 325, the Council of Nicea referred to it as "an ancient and canonical law" (Canon 13). The very word *viaticum* once designated the provisions or money a traveler took for the road *(via)*. But, here, it is not so much the traveler who takes the Eucharist for provision on the great voyage, but rather Christ who meets the believer and leads him to the Father's house.

Communion-as-viaticum seals for eternity, between Jesus and his followers, this common destiny which every communion expresses so marvelously. "He who eats my flesh and drinks my blood lives in me, and I live in him" (John 6:56), the Lord asserts. For Christians at the hour of death, this "abiding" in Christ reveals its ultimate consequences: it is then that they truly die with Jesus (2 Timothy 3:11), that they are buried with him (Romans 6:4; Colossians 2:12), that they prepare to rise with him (Ephesians 2:6; Colossians 2:13; 3:1) and be glorified with him (Romans 8:17): in a word, it is then that they associate their own exodus—their departure from this world of grief and their entrance into the kingdom of the Father's joy—with the exodus of Jesus. Each communion is a prayer: "Come, Lord Jesus!" But now, prayer is transformed into the joy of his presence: "We shall stay with the Lord for ever" (1 Thessalonians 4:17). Each communion is a promise of eternity: "Anyone who eats my flesh and drinks my blood has eternal life, and I shall raise him up on the last day" (John 6:54). But now, in proportion as the night of agony wears on, the dawn of resurrection arises. The Eucharist-as-viaticum is the last thanksgiving in time, before that of eternity begins. It is the final encounter with Christ in praise, before face-to-face vision in the Father's house.

*   *
*

Not merely one facet of the Eucharistic mystery, thanksgiving is its very center. Without it, there is no Mass.

He who presides gives thanks "as well as he can": that is how Justin characterized the Mass toward the middle of the second century (see p. 27). Unquestionably, the rubrics have since channeled the tumultuous tide of spontaneous praise between the shores of Preface and Eucharistic Prayer. But the dynamism of prayer remains the same. Since Christ said to his Church, "Take this, this is my body," that "as well as he can" has grown infinite. For the Church has now received power to offer, no longer just the universe and man who epitomizes it in his being, but him who is in himself "all honor and all glory" for the Father: Christ Jesus.

IV

The Eucharist as Sacrifice

SACRIFICE IN GENERAL

Sacrifice is one of the most frequently used words in man's religious vocabulary. Yet its meaning varies widely, depending on the religion and culture in question. There is a world of difference between the sacrifices a football player makes to get the pigskin, the financial sacrifices parents impose upon themselves for their children's education, the foundation sacrifices the Canaanites offered when raising the walls of their ramparts upon human victims, the funerary sacrifices of Egypt, and what we traditionally call "the holy sacrifice of the Mass."

Etymologically, the word *sacrifice* comes from *sacrum facere*, "to make something sacred." It is related to *consecrate*, which means "to make sacred by dedication to God." But we see immediately that in the framework of Yahwism, where the whole universe is consecrated to God—"to Yahweh belong earth and all it holds" (Psalm 24:1)—such a notion of consecration is ambiguous. For one offers God the firstfruits of the harvest (Deuteronomy 26:1-11) or the firstborn of human love (Exodus 13:11-16), not so that they may be consecrated to him, but, rather, because they already are. And not only the first-fruits belong to him, but the entire harvest as well; not only the firstborn is dedicated to him, but all the other children, too—along with their mother—for they are born of his blessing (Psalm 128:4). In a certain sense, we cannot offer God anything that does not already belong to him; we give him only what we have received: "All comes from you; from your own hand we have given [these offerings] to you" (1 Chronicles 29:14).

Then, too, definitions of sacrifice vary from author to author. "Sacrifice," states E. Masure, "is the expressive and, if possible, efficacious sign of man's willed and suppliant return to his God, who receives it."[1] "*Sacrificium*," we read in J. de Baciocchi, "denotes a homage rendered to God through the of-fering of an object *(oblatio)* which then undergoes some deter-mined treatment, usually destructive *(immolatio)*, designed to materialize its transfer to the domain of God."[2] According to J. Galot, "Sacrifice is an offering made to God in order to render him homage, to enter into communication with him, and to ob-tain his favor."[3] Saint Augustine defines it more simply: "A vis-ible sacrifice is the sacrament—that is, the sacred sign—of an invisible sacrifice."[4] These definitions are precious insofar as they enable us to determine the constants found in every sacri-fice; but some may seem questionable, since they have obviously been tailored to fit the sacrifice of Christ on the cross and at the last supper. Yet that very fact allows us to conclude that the Mass is indeed a sacrifice.

In certain primitive animistic religions, sacrifice was be-lieved to calm the aggressiveness of malefic spirits, who, once pacified, would leave humans alone. (No thought was given to good spirits, who, by definition, were favorable to man.)

In the Assyro-Babylonian religions, there was a consider-able variety of sacrifices: offerings of food or incense, libations

---

[1] *Le sacrifice du Chef*, p. 92.
[2] *L'Eucharistie* (Desclée & Cie, 1964), p. 54.
[3] *La rédemption, mystère d'alliance*, p. 112.
[4] *The City of God*, X, 5.

and blood sacrifices. Particularly interesting is the expiatory sacrifice, in which we find—with a prodigious diversity of expression—the principle of substitution. A victim was immolated so as to be delivered up to the devils tormenting a sinner or a sick person; thanks to potent incantations, these devils would freely or forcedly yield and enter into the animal.[5]

The Canaanites, whose sacrificial rites profoundly inspired Israel's, practiced human sacrifice. Israel was aware of such atrocities, which sacred hysteria tried to transform into homage to the divinity. For example, the Gibeonites (2 Samuel 21:1-14) demanded seven of Saul's sons and "impaled them on the mountain before Yahweh" (v. 9) as a fertility rite. Similarly, when the combined armies of Israel, Judah and Edom besieged the king of Moab in Kir-haresheth, "he took his eldest son . . . and offered him as a sacrifice on the city wall" (2 Kings 3:27). Eventually, Israel itself stooped to such aberrations. Thus we read of Ahaz (735-716) "copying the[se] shameful practices" and of Manasseh (687-642), who "caused his sons to pass through the fire in the Valley of Ben-hinnom."[6] But Yahwistic orthodoxy always rejected such practices as "abominations."[7]

Among the ancient Arabs, sacrifice required the shedding of the victim's blood. The blood itself, as a symbol of brotherhood, was used to seal the union existing between friends or with God; and the meal, especially if the guests ate the victim

---

[5]Here is a specimen of these incantations as it appears in R. de Vaux, *Studies in Old Testament Sacrifice* (Cardiff: University of Wales Press, 1964), p. 56:

A lamb is a substitute for man
he has given the lamb for his life,
he has given head of lamb for head of man
he has given neck of lamb for neck of man
he has given breast of lamb for breast of man.

[6]2 Chronicles 33:6; 2 Kings 16:3 and 21:6; see also Jeremiah 7:31 and 19:5; Ezekiel 16:21. (The Valley of Ben-hinnom was also called Gehinnom—the "Gehenna" of earlier translations and the symbolic name for hell in the New Testament.—Translator.)

[7]Deuteronomy 12:31; see also Leviticus 18:21 and 20:2-5; Deuteronomy 18:31. The story of Abraham's sacrifice (Genesis 22) teaches, at least implicitly, that God does not want to be honored by human sacrifice.

together, conferred a sacred character on their blood brotherhood. In Egypt, the daily sacrifice took on the nature of a meal offered to the divinity, with the worshipers holding a bloody thigh from the victim up to the mouth of the god's statue and daubing his lips with the gore. Such food offerings were also made in Chaldea, as Daniel 14:5 informs us.

Though some of these sacrifices offend our sensibilities, they are all venerable insofar as they represent the efforts of fear—and often of love—in search of the unknown God. They are hands extended in the night toward him whose name is yet a mystery. After all, man, left to his own devices, deals with the invisible as best he can.

Still, it is dangerous to proceed exclusively from such data in explaining Jesus' sacrifice. For we would then be interpreting it in terms of the sacrificial practice of men, whereas it must be understood in terms of God's ways and what he has revealed about his own love. Otherwise, we fall into popular versions of salvation history, which run pretty much like this: "Through sin, man disobeys God. God becomes angry and demands a victim in expiation. So he sacrifices his own Son, and this death assuages his anger. As for the Mass, it reproduces the whole drama symbolically." Now, that view of redemption is false: it reduces God's behavior to the human level—and lower yet. For what man, even with the heart of a beast, would exact the death of his son to appease his wrath? Then, would God, who revealed himself on Sinai as "a God of tenderness and compassion" (Exodus 34:6), want that? To understand Jesus' sacrifice on Calvary and at the last supper, therefore, we must—while using the lights offered by other religions—replant it in biblical ground. Only there will we find the key to it.

BIBLICAL SACRIFICES

Biblical tradition lists three principal kinds of sacrifice: the holocaust, the communion sacrifice and the sacrifice of reparation.

The holocaust

The term *holocaust* comes to us, through the Septuagint and then the Vulgate, from the Hebrew *'olah*, whose root means "to ascend." This was the sacrifice in which the victim—a bull, a young goat, a lamb, or a turtledove and a pigeon—"ascended" to the altar, was entirely burned there and thus "ascended" as smoke toward God. The ritual[8] specified that the offerer was to lay his hand on the victim's head as a solemn gesture denoting that the animal was indeed his own and that he himself was offering it. Pouring out its blood on the borders of the altar was the duty of the priests. Along with this sacrifice went an offering (*minhah*) of wheaten flour kneaded in oil, and a libation of wine. In very early times, it expressed thanksgiving (cf. 1 Samuel 6:14) or petition, too (cf. 1 Samuel 7:9); and Leviticus gives it expiatory value. The complete burning of the victim aptly signified the totality and irrevocability of the gift.

The communion sacrifice

In Hebrew, this sacrifice was called *zebah shelamim*, or simply *zebah* or *shelamim*—terms which can be translated variously, since the nomenclature of sacrifice was somewhat fluid. *Zebah* designated any blood sacrifice accompanied by a religious meal. Semantically, *shelamim* is susceptible of several interpretations: it may be a peace offering, a plea for one's welfare, or a tribute intended to establish or reestablish relations with God—in other words, a covenant sacrifice. The victims were the same as for the holocaust, though birds were excluded; in compensation, the victims here could be female, whereas the holocaust required that they be male. There was the same imposition of the hand and the same pouring of the blood on the altar. But the chief characteristic was that the victim was not

---

[8]Cf. Leviticus 1-7. This is the sacrificial ritual of the second Temple. Having received its definitive form only after the return from exile, it reflects some fairly late practices together with very ancient ones.

wholly burned, but shared three ways: among God, the priest and the offerer. Besides the blood, God was given the fat, which was considered a noble part and burned: "All the fat belongs to Yahweh. . . . Never eat either fat or blood" (Leviticus 3:17). This communion meal, where the believer received his share of the victim offered on the altar, sealed, so to speak, the "familial" community of God with his people. In this sense, Paul would later say that "those who eat the sacrifices are in communion with the altar" and that being in communion with the altar means entering into communion with God (1 Corinthians 10:18-20).

This sacrifice was festive and joyous. The watchword was "rejoicing before Yahweh" (Deuteronomy 14:26), the altar became "the table of Yahweh" (Ezekiel 44:16; Malachi 1:7, 12), and the ritual offerings were "the food of Yahweh" (Leviticus 21:6, 8; 22:25; Numbers 28:2; Ezekiel 44:7). Also placed before him were loaves of bread (Leviticus 24:5-9), oil and wine (Numbers 15:1-12), as well as salt, the seasoning for the meal (Leviticus 2:13; Ezekiel 43:24). And the pleasant aroma from the dishes, gratifying Yahweh's nostrils, ascended to heaven as "an appeasing fragrance" (Numbers 28:2; cf. Leviticus 1:9, 13; Exodus 29:18, 25; Genesis 8:21). Of course, as Yahwistic orthodoxy well knew, Israel's transcendent God was not to be compared to the stupid gods in the Canaanite pantheon, who had to be fed little mouthfuls like infants. In fact, the people delighted in ridiculing the celestial rabble of whom Utnapishtim, the Babylonian Noah, relates:

> I offered a sacrifice.
> I poured out a libation on the top of the mountain. . . .
> The gods smelled the savor,
> The gods smelled the sweet savor,
> The gods crowded like flies about the sacrificer.[9]

---

[9] *The Epic of Gilgamesh*, XI, 155-161, in J. B. Pritchard, *The Ancient Near East, an Anthology of Texts and Pictures* (Princeton University Press, 1958), p. 70.

And in Psalm 50:12-13, Yahweh himself, with a sort of amused irony, protests:

> If I were hungry, I should not tell you,
> since the world and all it holds is mine.
> Do I eat the flesh of bulls,
> or drink goats' blood?

But, even though God does not eat, the communion sacrifice admirably expresses conviviality with him: it is a meal taken in his presence, the altar is the common table, and the believer is God's guest.

The sacrifice of reparation

Hebrew used two terms for the sacrifice of reparation:
—*Hattat*, which denoted at one and the same time sin, sacrifice for sin, and the victim of this sacrifice. (The ritual is found in Leviticus 4:1 to 5:13 and 6:17-23.)
—*Asam*, which likewise denoted the offense, the means of atoning for it, and the sacrifice of reparation. (The ritual is found in Leviticus 5:14-16 and 7:1-6.)
In point of fact, the difference between sacrifices of reparation and sacrifices for sin is fairly hazy. Leviticus 7:7 even states that the rites were identical. Some scholars opine that "the *hattat* covers a wider field, and that the *asam* is specially concerned with the faults by which God (or His priests) or the neighbor have been frustrated, which gives to this sacrifice its reparation character."[10] The confusion between both sacrifices may date back to Leviticus' last redactors, who either discriminated two originally similar terms or confounded two different ones.
What characterized the rite of reparation was the importance accorded to the blood. Thus, in the sacrifice offered for "the assembly of the children of Israel"—that is, for the whole nation (Leviticus 4:13-21)—the priest collected the blood, carried a little of it into the holy of holies, sprinkled the veil "be-

---

[10]R. de Vaux, *op. cit.*, p. 100.

fore Yahweh" (v. 17) seven times, put some on the horns of the altar of incense, and then poured out the rest at the foot of the altar of holocaust. Indeed, the blood was considered the victim's "soul," his very life (Genesis 9:4; Deuteronomy 12:23), and had expiatory value: "The life of the flesh is in the blood. This blood I myself have given you to perform the rite of atonement for your lives at the altar; for it is blood that atones for life" (Leviticus 17:11).

JESUS' SACRIFICE AT THE LAST SUPPER AND ON THE CROSS

The vocabulary of sacrifice stamps the thinking of the early community in regard to Christ's death. This is the sacrifice of the servant of Yahweh, who gives his life as ransom for the multitude (p. 42); of the paschal lamb at the messianic feast (p. 43); of the new covenant, which fulfills that of Sinai (p.9). Paul boldly asserts, "For our sake God made the sinless one into sin *[hattat]*"—that is, the victim for sin (2 Corinthians 5:21). And John, for his part, says, "He is the sacrifice that takes our sins away" (1 John 2:2; cf. 4:10). These statements are directly related to the text from the last supper: Jesus' blood "is to be poured out for many for the forgiveness of sins" (Matthew 26:28). How so? For the holocaust of Jesus is more like some unspeakable butchery than a sacrifice offered to God. How shall we see, in the slaughter on Golgotha, the sacrifice for forgiveness of sins and the gift of the Father's love?

Here, we have to follow humbly along the paths of Old Testament ritual and read of Jesus' death with the eyes of Scripture. True, it does not fit neatly into any of the ancient categories of sacrifice, yet each category further unveils the fullness of its mystery. Jesus' death is a holocaust if we consider the irrevocability of the immolation; but, here, the victim rises again! It is a communion sacrifice if we consider the covenant meal inaugurated at the last supper; but, here, the victim is also the principal offerer! It is a sacrifice of reparation for sin; but, here, the victim is invaded by heavenly glory and seated at the right hand of the Father! Christ's sacrifice, therefore, is singular

and irreducible; it transcends all the ancient sacrificial categories and realizes the spiritual fullness of holocaust, communion
sacrifice and sacrifice of reparation. St. Paul states that Christ
gave himself up "in our place as a fragrant offering and a sacrifice to God" (Ephesians 5:2). How is that to be understood?

The ritual of the Day of Atonement

On the Day of Atonement, *Yom Hakkippurim* (Leviticus
16), the high priest used to offer a bull in sacrifice *(kipper)* as a
ransom *(koper)* for sin. Then—the only time during the year—
he would enter beyond the veil of the holy of holies, incense the
propitiatory *(kapporeth)*, and sprinkle it with blood seven times.
This propitiatory—also called the altar of propitiation or the
throne of mercy—was a plaque of pure gold resting on the ark
of the covenant between two golden cherubs. As the "throne of
Yahweh" (Leviticus 16:2; 1 Samuel 4:4), who, the psalmist says,
was "enthroned on the cherubs" (Psalm 80:2), it was the place
from which he spoke to Moses (Exodus 25:22; Numbers 7:89),
manifested his mercy and revealed his Word (the Vulgate often
translates *kapporeth* by *oraculum*). It remained empty, as if to
signify the residence of the invisible God among his people.
After the exile, it was considered the substitute for the ark.

The original meaning of the root *kpr* (the base of *kapporeth*: propitiatory) seems to have been "to wipe," "to clean."
Thus, when Jacob wanted to appease the anger of his brother
Esau, who was marching against him with an armed band, he
sent him a present, thinking, "I shall wipe his face by sending
him a gift in advance; so when I come face to face with him, he
may perhaps receive me favorably" (Genesis 32:21, Hebrew).
To wipe or clean someone's face was to make it propitious, favorable, welcoming, reconciling. Of God we can say that he
"wipes away" sin, that he effaces it from sight (cf. Jeremiah
18:23); and we pray to him, "Though our faults overpower us,
you blot them out" (Psalm 65:3). So, on the Day of Atonement,
at the ritual of the *kapporeth*, God's face was cleaned, wiped,
appeased. Then the light of his face would smile anew on his
people (cf. Psalm 67:1).

On 'hat same day, the community presented two goats—one allotted to Yahweh and the other to Azazel, a famous demon who, according to popular belief, lived somewhere in the desert. Lots were drawn, and the goat whose lot was marked "For Azazel" was set before Yahweh. The high priest placed his hands upon it, loading it with all the sins of the community, then chased it out to carry their sins away to Azazel's desert home. As for the goat whose lot was marked "For Yahweh," it was sacrificed, and the high priest again sprinkled the propitiatory with its blood. Partly archaic and folkloric, these rites signified transference of sins, with forgiveness and purification—in a word, reentry into the state of holiness befitting the nation consecrated to Yahweh.

In his letter to the Hebrews, Paul uses the Day of Atonement ritual to explain Jesus' sacrifice. First, he posits what seems an incontestable axiom: "If there is no shedding of blood, there is no remission" (Hebrews 9:22)—which is patently false. For, being so well versed in Scripture, he surely realizes there are other means of forgiveness, like penance, prayer and almsgiving, not to mention ritual means, like offering wheaten flour for sin in lieu of a victim (Leviticus 5:11-13). But since the cross was a bloody sacrifice, he heavily underscores the importance of blood, which makes atonement. He explains: "But now Christ has come, as the high priest of all blessings which were to come. He has passed through the greater, the more perfect tent, which is better than the one made by men's hands because it is not of this created order; and he has entered the sanctuary once and for all, taking with him not the blood of goats and bull calves, but his own blood, having won an eternal redemption for us" (Hebrews 9:11-12). The sacrifice of the cross, therefore, was the messianic community's own *Yom Hakkippurim*—the day of forgiveness "once and for all": for, whereas the high priest had to repeat the sprinkling of the *kapporeth* every year, thus implying that past sacrifices were imperfect, Christ "made his appearance once and for all . . . to do away with sin by sacrificing himself" (Hebrews 9:26). Furthermore, the ancient ritual brought out the true meaning of God's forgiveness. The slaughtering of the victim was not designed to punish an offender and placate a vengeful God with blood. This was the blood, not of death, but of life; and the *kapporeth* was drenched in it to signify that communion of life was reestablished between God and men, that the covenant was restored as on Sinai: "This is the blood of the covenant which God has formed with you." Our modern sensibilities may be somewhat jarred when Scripture says blood "washes" and "purifies," since we would be more inclined to say it spots. When Revelation 7:14 tells us, "These are the people who have been through the great persecution and . . . have washed their robes white again in the blood of the Lamb," we must understand that these pilgrims of the final persecution have been fully forgiven, "wiped clean," because they have been plunged, as it were, into the blood—meaning: into the life—of Jesus.

Consequently, Christ was immolated, not through vengeance on our sins, so as to "allay" God's "anger," but rather for our sins—that is, in order to "wipe them away," forgive them, inundate us with his life in his blood, give it to us "to the full" (John 10:10). He was not the scapegoat burdened with our sins and crushed under the curse of God. In the *Yom Hakkippurim* ritual, that goat was impure and therefore unsuitable for sacrifice: it was the devil's and was marked "For Azazel." Christ, on the contrary, exists "For God" and liberates us by his precious blood, like that of a lamb "without spot or stain" (1 Peter 1:19).

The propitiatory in the new covenant

After stating that believers "are justified . . . by being redeemed in Christ Jesus," Paul adds, "God put him forward as a propitiatory [*hilasterion*, the Greek for *kapporeth*] through faith, by his blood" (Romans 3:24-25, literal translation). The sentence is a trifle awkward, as often happens when Paul wants to say too much all at once. But the comparison is very beautiful and shows Jesus as the new *kapporeth*, where the rite of messianic pardon is accomplished. The old propitiatory was Yahweh's throne, the site of his revelation *(oraculum)* to the community of the children of Israel, the place whence forgive-

ness came. Jesus, the propitiatory of the messianic sanctuary, is
the pulpit from which the Father speaks, the throne from which
he extends his definitive rule over men; from his body flows forgiveness for sins. The old propitiatory was sprinkled with the
blood of the victim on which the lot "For God" had fallen.
Jesus, of course, belongs for ever to his Father, he bathes his
own body in the blood poured out on the cross, and that blood
is life for those who believe. The sprinkling of the *kapporeth*
took place behind the veil, in the shadows of the holy of holies,
where the high priest entered alone once a year. But the sprinkling of Christ's blood takes place on the stage of the world; the
new propitiatory is exposed on the cross in the sight of mankind; and his bleeding wounds, transformed into a source of life
by the resurrection, are always in the Father's presence "to intercede" in our behalf (Hebrews 7:25).

The spiritual sacrifice

We must underline the spiritual aspect of Jesus' sacrifice.
In point of fact, Christ was killed by men's hatred. The ex-
ecutioners who carried out the sentence certainly had no inten-
tion of immolating a victim, but simply crucifying a wrongdoer.
Where, then, was his sacrifice? Can one change a murder into a
holocaust? Can the executioner's hatred become the thanksgiving of the doomed?
To tell the truth, such questions can be raised with regard
to any sacrifice, for any sacrifice can be drained of its spiritual
significance and reduced to a purely external rite. Now, a ritual
gesture has meaning only if it expresses the devotion of the soul.
What constitutes a sacrifice is not the victim offered—a slaught-
ered goat is worth nothing to God—but the offering of the victim: I mean the inner sentiments of the offerer. God judges man
by the heart, not by the weight of the victims or the smoke from
the fat. Nowhere does Scripture limit sacrifice to external rites.
Instead, it ceaselessly recalls the primacy of the heart over the
outward act: mercy is better than sacrifice (Hosea 6:6; Matthew
9:13; 12:7), submissiveness better than the fat of rams (1 Samu-

el 15:22), the contrite soul and the humbled spirit better than thousands of fattened lambs (Daniel 3:39), justice and integrity better than chanting and strumming on harps (Amos 5:21-24), aid to orphans and widows better than holocausts (Isaiah 1:11-17), loving tenderly and walking humbly before God better than torrents of oil poured out in libation (Micah 6:7-8), reconciliation with a brother better than offerings (Matthew 5:23), and mutual forgiveness better than lip prayer (Mark 11:25). Scripture (Psalm 51:16-17) formulates the rule for sacrifice thus:

> Sacrifice gives you no pleasure;
> were I to offer holocaust, you would not have it.
> God's sacrifice is this broken spirit,
> you will not scorn this crushed and broken heart, O God.

Not that the external sacrifice is refused, but it has significance only if it expresses the offering of the heart.

Now, that is precisely where the greatness of Jesus' sacrifice lay. His whole life was an offering. The letter to the Hebrews (10:5-8, quoting Psalm 40:7-9) does not hesitate to assert that the incarnation signalized the end of the old sacrifices and their replacement by obedience:

> This is what [Christ] said, on coming into the world:
> "You, who wanted no sacrifice or oblation,
> prepared a body for me.
> You took no pleasure in holocausts or sacrifices for sin;
> then I said,
> just as I was commanded in the scroll of the book,
> 'God, here I am! I am coming to obey your will.' "

That affirmation, "I am coming to obey your will," was the base on which Jesus built his own life. Merging into the loving obedience of his "Yes, Father, for that is your good pleasure" (Matthew 11:26), which quintessentialized his religion of praise, it transfigured each moment of his existence into an offering of love. Exteriorly, his was the life of any Nazarene, any Israelite carpenter of his day. Only the heart was more beautiful: it was open onto heaven and lived wholly on the love of God: "I do always what pleases him" (John 8:29). Just as we nourish our bodies on bread to subsist, he nourished his soul on praise and obedience: "My food is to do the will of the one who sent me" (John 4:34). And if our lives sometimes reveal their secretest meaning at the hour of death, Jesus' life proved a holocaust of love in an infinite radiance of peace and trust, changing the gates of death into a door of hope: "Father, into your hands I commit my spirit" (Luke 23:46). Contemplating his death, the letter to the Hebrews states, "Through the eternal Spirit, he offered himself as the perfect sacrifice to God" (9:14).

We need the last supper to understand Calvary better. In truth, that supper was the prophetic announcement of Jesus' death. It concluded the other announcements, which, from Tabor to Jerusalem, had transformed his life into a path to Golgatha. It was the most urgent, for the cross was drawing near. And the most significant also, for the death it foretold was not the biblical ideal of departing from this world filled with days and surrounded by children from the third and fourth generations, in order to rest with one's fathers, but, instead, a violent death—that of the servant of Yahweh crushed by suffering, that of a paschal lamb being led to slaughter. His blood would flow like the wine poured out at the feast, and his body would be broken like the unleavened bread torn for the guests. Thus, the last supper was the "acting out" of Christ's death on Calvary.

This prophetic gesture fit perfectly into the tradition of Israel, where the prophets predicted the future not only through oracles but also through symbolic gestures. So, when Sargon captured Ashdod in 711, Isaiah walked around naked and barefoot to presage the discomfiture of those who were relying on Egypt (Isaiah 20:1-6); Jeremiah smashed a jug, declaring, "Yahweh Sabaoth says this: 'I am going to break this people and this city just as one breaks a potter's pot, irreparably' " (Jeremiah 19:10-11); and Ezekiel mimed departure into exile to announce the captivity of Israel (Ezekiel 12:1-10).

Now, in Israelitic thought, predicting future events was definitive proof that Yahweh is indeed the lord of history. He can foretell the future, because he holds it in his hand; he shapes history, makes it move ahead through his "days," ravages it with his anger, lulls it with his tenderness, and molds the clay of human history like the potter at his wheel (Isaiah 64:8). This divine omnipotence is exercised particularly over human life: he keeps our soul "close in the satchel of life" (1 Samuel 25:29), and we can well say, "My days are in your hand" (Psalm 31:15). Consequently, when Jesus predicted his sacrificial death, he declared himself lord of history. He did not undergo his passion: he took charge of it and transformed it into a voluntary offering. "Knowing everything that was going to happen to him" (John 18:4), he could state with a sovereign majesty that dominated death, "I lay down my life in order to take it up again. No one takes it from me; I lay it down of my own free will" (John 10:17-18).

The sacrifice accepted by God

How do we know when God accepts a sacrifice? For, unless he does, the victim is just a corpse and "the prayer and entreaty, aloud and in silent tears" (Hebrews 5:7), remain a monologue in a desert of suffering.

In holocausts, the smoke which rose heavenward was supposed to form the link between this world and the kingdom of God: "This will be a burned offering whose fragrance will appease Yahweh" (Exodus 29:18). Flame, too, could become the road to heaven. The greatest grace in Manoah's life was to witness this marvel while offering a holocaust to announce the birth of Samson: "As the flame went up heavenwards from the altar, the angel of Yahweh [that is, God himself] ascended in the flame in the sight of Manoah and his wife" (Judges 13:20)— an obvious sign that his sacrifice was accepted. Again, when Gideon offered sacrifice, the angel of Yahweh touched the offerings with the staff in his hand and caused the fire for the holocaust to burst forth (Judges 6:21). Unique in the history of holocausts was the sign with which God marked Elijah's on Mount Carmel: onto an altar drenched with water, he sent fire from heaven to consume the sacrifice (1 Kings 18:38), thus showing his acceptance of his servant's offering in the sight of all Israel and Baal's priestlings.

In Jesus' sacrifice, the fire from heaven was the Spirit, the "breath" of life, who resurrected the crucified Christ. The resurrection was the official seal by which the Father signified that he accepted Jesus' offering, that he freed him "from the pangs of Hades" (Acts 2:24), that he received into his loving arms him who had made himself into sin *(hattat)* for his brothers. He not only accepted but—what is more—glorified him, proclaiming him "Son of God in all his power . . . in the order of the spirit, the spirit of holiness" (cf. Romans 1:4), making him "both Lord and Christ" (Acts 2:36), and giving him "all authority in heaven and on earth" (Matthew 28:18). Paul explains: "[The Father] used [the strength of his power] to raise him from the dead and to make him sit at his right hand, in heaven."[11] Just now, I mentioned the Old Testament scene in which Manoah and his wife, intoxicated with miracles, contemplated the angel of Yahweh "ascending" in the flame from the holocaust. The other half of that diptych is the ascension, where the Twelve, symbolizing the tribes of Israel, saw Jesus "taken up into heaven, at the right hand of God" (Mark 16:19). The ascension was the Father's "yes" to his Son's sacrifice. It was heaven's reply to the words of the Crucified: "Father, into your hands I commit my spirit."

Here again, the last supper must not be separated from the cross, for the supper prophesied the resurrection and the ascension, opened Jesus' death upon eternity, and announced beforehand that the Father accepted his sacrifice. Indeed, as we have seen (p. 61), the passover was oriented toward the eternal feast. It was not the last passover he would celebrate with his disciples, but simply the last on earth. For the day will come when he will once more drink the new wine in the kingdom; the eternal feast will dawn at which the passover will be "fulfilled." A farewell meal, the last supper is also a feast of hope. Between it and the day he returns, there is the Father's official accep-

---

[11]Ephesians 1:19-20. In Pauline theology, it is always the Father (Romans 1:4; 4:24; 10:9; 1 Corinthians 6:14; 15:15; 2 Corinthians 3:14; Colossians 2:12; Ephesians 1:19-20; Galatians 1:1; 1 Thessalonians 1:10), his glory (Romans 6:4) or his power (2 Corinthians 13:4) which resurrects Jesus. This faithfully reflects the primitive kerygma (Acts 2:24).

tance of the sacrifice, as signified by the establishing of Jesus' universal lordship.

THE SACRIFICE OF THE MASS

"To do this" in memory of Jesus is to renew his actions at the last supper, while giving them the same sacrificial dimension. It may seem trite, therefore, to say that the Mass is a memorial sacrifice. Unfortunately, after centuries of theological tranquility, the peace of that affirmation was troubled by the discussions, and sometimes the disputes, of the Protestant Reformation and the Catholic Counter-Reformation. The echo of those encounters has come down to our own day. A word must be said about them here.

It can be stated that the princes of the Reformation—Luther, Zwingli and Calvin—all accepted the Mass as a thanksgiving sacrifice but rejected it as a propitiatory sacrifice in the way Catholic tradition then understood it. Luther's starting point was his attack on "works" which sought to earn justification by themselves. Accordingly, in the *Articles of Schmalkalden* (February, 1537), he first posited the unique role of Christ the Redeemer and justification by faith alone—a position which permitted him to conclude, "Within papism, the Mass is the grossest and most horrible abomination, fundamentally and diametrically opposed to the first article." Elsewhere, in his *De abroganda missa privata* (1521), he declared that "the Masses which are called sacrifices are the height of idolatry and impiety" *("summam idolatriam et impietatem")*. The violence of his attacks stems from the fact that he considered the Mass as the keystone of Roman Catholicism: "They know perfectly well that if the Mass falls, papism will fall." One may regret the enormity of certain statements—the Mass being an invention of the devil, for example—and explain it by the ardor of polemics in those days, but it does not clarify the discussion.[12]

---

[12]See J. Rivière, *La messe durant la période de la Réforme et du Concile de Trente*, in *Dictionnaire de théologie catholique (D.T.C.)*, Vol. 10, col. 1085-1142; and the articles by H. Grass, "Luther et la liturgie eucharistique," and T. Suess, "L'aspect sacrificiel de la sainte Cène à la lumière de la tradition luthérienne," in *Eucharisties d'Orient et d'Occident*, pp. 135-150 and 151-170.

These attacks readily found sympathetic ears. Abuses, like some hideous leprosy, were gnawing at Christian practice and battering the faith of the unlearned. The Council of Trent admitted them straight out, condemning the superstition which invested the Mass with quasi-magical expiatory power, the avarice of priests haggling over the Mass, the senseless number of low Masses which multiplied, not devotion, but stipends (Luther, in 1525, spoke of "the horror of the low Mass": *"Vom Greuel der Stillmesse"*)—to say nothing of the indecent celebrations, the profane songs, the drinking bouts, and so forth. None of this necessarily pertained to dogma, but it did explain the crisis. We may note, furthermore, that the Church would accede to Protestant demands for the use of the vernacular, communion under both kinds, and liturgical renewal. Unfortunately, this was not done at Trent, but—four centuries later—at Vatican II.

On September 17, 1562, the Council of Trent adopted the text on "The Institution of the Sacrosanct Sacrifice of the Mass." In a taut, tumultuous, inordinately long sentence—as if to compass the truth and block the road to error—it affirmed (1) the unicity and the perennialness of the sacrifice on the cross; (2) its perpetuation in the Church by a visible rite; (3) the first offering of the Eucharistic sacrifice at the last supper; and (4) the command to repeat it given to the apostles and their successors. Here, paragraphed for convenience' sake, is that famous text:

> (1) He, therefore, our God and Lord, though He was about to offer Himself once to God the Father upon the altar of the Cross by the mediation of death, so that He might accomplish an eternal redemption for them,
> (2) nevertheless, that His sacerdotal office might not come to an end with His death at the Last Supper, on the night He was betrayed, so that He might leave to His beloved spouse the Church a visible sacrifice (as the nature of man demands), whereby that bloody sacrifice once to be completed on the Cross might be represented, and the memory of it remain even to the end of the world and its saving grace be applied to the remission of those sins which we daily commit,
> (3) declaring Himself constituted "a priest forever according to the order of Melchisedech," offered to God the

Father His own body and blood under the species of bread and wine, and under the symbol of those same things gave to the apostles (whom He then constituted priests of the New Testament), so that they might partake,

(4) and He commanded them and their successors in the priesthood in these words to make offering: "Do this in commemoration of me, etc.," as the Catholic Church has always understood and taught.[13]

This text voiced the belief of the Church at a given period in her history, in the language of that period, and for the needs of that period—most especially, to confront the Protestant crisis. It would serve as a theological basis for the Counter-Reformation.

Vatican II did not choose to repeat Trent's title ("The Sacrosanct Sacrifice of the Mass") but preferred to speak more simply of "The Mystery of the Eucharist." It quotes Trent—but from memory, so to speak; it simplifies the exposition while yet broadening the perspectives:

At the Last Supper, on the night when He was betrayed, our Savior instituted the Eucharistic Sacrifice of His Body and Blood. He did this in order to perpetuate the sacrifice of the Cross throughout the centuries until He should come again, and so to entrust to His beloved spouse, the Church, a memorial of His death and resurrection: a sacrament of love, a sign of unity, a bond of charity, a paschal banquet in which Christ is consumed, the mind is filled with grace, and a pledge of future glory is given to us.[14]

In asserting the sacrificial character of the Mass, neither Trent nor Vatican II intends to close the debate. On the contrary, it is still wide open, for they do not say *how* the Mass is a sacrifice or even specify what a sacrifice *is*. Melanchthon, commenting on the *Augsburg Confession*, had ample reason to storm against the vague terminology and "the immense tumult

---

[13]Denzinger, *The Sources of Catholic Dogma*, translated by Roy J. Deferrari from the 13th edition of *Enchiridion Symbolorum* (St. Louis: B. Herder Book Company, 1957), No. 938, pp. 288-289.

[14]*Constitution on the Sacred Liturgy*, 47.

of words" *("ingens tumultus verborum")* in this area. There is need of further theological reflection, therefore, since conciliar definitions are not pillows to sleep on but, rather, guides to help us better understand the data of the faith.

I do not intend to add new pages to these discussions but, instead, to point out a few essential truths which can serve as anchorage for the affirmation of the faith.

The unicity and transcendence of Christ's sacrifice

The first and most urgent point is to recall the transcendence of Christ and the unicity of his redemptive act. In other words, the Mass adds nothing either to Christ or to his sacrifice: one is the priest, one is the sacrifice.

"There is only one mediator between God and mankind, himself a man, Christ Jesus" (1 Timothy 2:5). The unicity of Christ's mediation is such that his priesthood transcends all others; it is the brilliance of a light so dazzling that it absorbs every other light. When the New Testament began, the levitical priesthood ceased; and, in the new covenant, Jesus has no successors. (Those who follow after him are called "presbyters" or "elders," and do not continue the Old Testament priesthood.)

The transcendence of his priesthood is explained, not principally by the perfection of the sacrifice he offers, but first and foremost by what he is. Indeed, he himself is the very covenant which he seals between heaven and earth; for in the oneness of his person he unites the dust of humanity and the fire of divinity, in the mystery of his being he transforms our humanity into a song of praise—into Eucharist. His priestly action is nothing other than the anointing of his humanity by his divinity, and the heart of the Virgin Mary was the temple for this "ordination," in which the "Son of Man" became priest in becoming "Son of God." He is the only priest because he is the only Son. His priesthood is the very source of the priestly character of the New Testament people. What grace of mediation could be added to such a priesthood, or subtracted from it, by any priest?

Unique also is his sacrifice. Here, we must recall the

famous *hapax*, "only once," "once and for all," in Paul's letter
to the Hebrews: "[Christ] has made his appearance *once and for
all*, now at the end of the last age, to do away with sin by
sacrificing himself" (9:26), "[he] offers himself *only once*"
(9:28), "he has entered the sanctuary *once and for all*" (9:12), so
that we may "be made holy by the offering of his body made
once and for all" (10:10). The perfection of his sacrifice is to-
kened by the resurrection and the ascension, which the letter to
the Hebrews calls his entrance into the heavenly Tent. In previous holocausts, the smoke which rose toward heaven was a
prayer: man implored God to accept his offering signified by the
victim. Here, the offerer himself is received into heaven. His is
the only sacrifice, because he is the only Son of God. What new
oblational value could be added to such a sacrifice, or subtracted from it, by any Mass?

We must proclaim—unto satiety!—the absolute transcendence of Christ Jesus. The Father has but one Son. He is "the
Son that he loves" (Colossians 1:13): "This is my Son, the
Beloved; my favour rests on him" (Matthew 3:17). In other
words, the Father's goodwill is extended only to those whose
faces reproduce the features of the Beloved; he can accept only
such offerings as are presented by this one hand he loves. Outside of Jesus, there is neither priesthood nor offering. Not only
must we resign ourselves joyously to this impossibility of adoring God outside of the only Son, but we should wholeheartedly
bless the Father, for if our offering resembles that of Jesus,
then, "through him and in him," we too can, like well-beloved
sons, give thanks to God. And the Father will recognize his
Son's voice through ours, and his Son's sacrifice in the offering
presented by our hands. Such is the prime reality of the Mass.

The sacramental actualization of Christ's sacrifice

In speaking of the "sacramental actualization" of Christ's
sacrifice, we are not attempting to explain the mystery, but simply to give it some sort of name. For the mystery—how this actualization is effected—remains intact, whatever name we give

it. We are merely trying to situate it. Indeed, what can we do before the mystery of God but stammer like children?

The word *sacramental* is used in order to affirm that Christ instituted the Mass as a visible sign of grace, that it is celebrated in compliance with his command to "do this" as a memorial of him. Surely, we Christians should actualize the Lord's sacrifice our whole life long, amid the burdens and joys of each day. Have we not been plunged by baptism (Romans 6:3-4) into his death and resurrection? But, here, we do so by celebrating the Lord's Supper as we have been asked.

The word *actualization* is used in order to affirm that the Mass is a certain re-presentation—that is to say, the act of making Jesus' sacrifice present again. St. Thomas, the prince of precise theological terminology, states with wisely calculated imprecision that the Mass is "a certain representative image of the passion of Christ."[15] It is not a repetition of the cross: to actualize does not mean to begin anew, but to render present that which already exists. Neither is it a complement, as if it brought forth new motives for reconciliation or thanksgiving: to actualize does not mean to complete. We should speak, rather, of an unfolding in time and space, for each ecclesial community, of this sacrifice which transcends time and, through the resurrection, is placed in God's eternity. Just as Christ is contemporaneous with all ages, so his sacrifice dominates the flux of world history; every age is brought face to face with the cross and beckoned by its grace. The sacrificial and Eucharistic value of Christ's death remains eternally self-identical: infinite; but every age comes to draw from it by celebrating the Lord's supper. At Mass, there is nothing new on Christ's part; what is new is the Church's participation, what changes is the new hands reaching toward the cross both to receive forgiveness and to express thanks.

One could also suggest this image: just as a parched traveler does not change the well by slaking his thirst there, and just as a shivering pauper does not enrich the sun by warming him-

---

[15]"*Imago quaedam est repraesentativa passionis Christi,*" *Summa Theologica,* Part III, ques. 83, art. 1.

self in its rays, so—and in the same manner—the number of Masses offered does not change anything in Christ, but changes everything in us. They add up among themselves, but do not add to the cross; they enrich the Church, not the Lord. They do not cut Christ's sacrifice into countless secondary sacrifices, but, rather, attest to its unicity, its efficacity, its transcendence. Vatican II states that priests "re-present and apply in the Sacrifice of the Mass the one sacrifice of the New Testament, namely the sacrifice of Christ offering Himself once and for all to His Father as a spotless victim."[16] Thus, the Council of Trent can assert that each Mass is a sacrifice, and Vatican II can add that Christ's is "the one sacrifice of the New Testament," because each Mass is the sacramental actualization of this one sacrifice.

Is the Mass, then, nothing but a heart thrown open to God? Does he not intervene in some special way? Yes, he acts, and so does the Church. The Church is at work insofar as she performs a sacramental act: offering God her thanksgiving at the Lord's supper. And God is at work insofar as he gives that act a sacramental efficacy. For he alone, through his grace, can transform the bread of earth into the bread of heaven, change an ordinary table into the altar of God, and transfigure a friendship meal into the Lord's supper. Let us draw another comparison: just as each Mass multiplies the number of consecrated hosts, but not the Christ present in them, so each Mass multiplies the number of sacramental actualizations of Christ's sacrifice, but not the one sacrifice itself. All the same, each Mass requires the intervention of God's omnipotence.

The Church's specific task is to present the bread and the wine for the sacrificial meal and implore God to send his Spirit to transubstantiate them. That is what she does in the epiclesis which introduces the account of the institution:

Let your Spirit come upon these gifts to make them holy,
so that they may become for us
the body and blood of our Lord, Jesus Christ.[17]

---

[16]Dogmatic Constitution on the Church, 28.

[17]Eucharistic Prayer II. The epicleses in Prayers III and IV are almost identical with this one.

God's specific action is to answer the Church's prayer, as he has promised, by consecrating the bread and the wine of the Lord's supper.

Then the Church, rich with the sacramental presence of Christ, can present "her" sacrifice to the Father:

> We offer you his body and blood,
> the acceptable sacrifice
> which brings salvation to the whole world.
> Lord, look upon this sacrifice
> which you have given to your Church . . .
> Look with favor on your Church's offering,
> and see the victim
> whose death has reconciled us to yourself.[18]

THE MASS IN OUR LIVES

I have stressed the transcendence of Christ's sacrifice. But that does not mean overlooking its immanence at the heart of our lives. Quite the contrary. The Church who offers becomes the Church who offers herself. She cannot offer the Father anything except Jesus alone; but the point is that, in this sacrifice, she can offer herself, along with the whole world. As the head of the body and the firstborn of the sons of God, Christ draws all of mankind along in the dynamism of his offering. That is the idea I want to underscore now.

Deviations

Two deviations imperil a proper understanding of the Church's participation in her Lord's sacrifice. The first emphasizes man's offering almost to the point of substituting it for— or at least overshadowing—Christ's. The offertory, with its mystique blown way out of proportion, afforded ample scope for the expression of such errors. Lest the faithful seem to be approaching God empty-handed, they would offer him whatever

---

[18]Eucharistic Prayers IV and III.

might symbolize human joy and suffering. There were touching
excesses. For example, in France, on the feast of Saint Fiacre,
the patron of market-gardeners, wagonloads of vegetables were
brought into the sanctuary; on the feast of Saint Barbara, piles
of miners' lamps; and on Armistice Day, forests of flags donated by veterans. More prosaically, the Sunday collection was offered to God after being carried in procession to the altar. To be
sure, the very word *offertory*—fortunately deleted from the new
Order of the Mass—as well as certain prayers accompanying it,
encouraged such misconceptions. These ceremonies at the offertory were most vulnerable, for it was easy to demonstrate that
God had no need of vegetables or lamps or flags. As a result,
there arose an "offertory crisis" which has not yet been totally
resolved. The situation is all the more painful since the offertory
possesses a potent affective charge and the gesture of offering
springs instinctively from the human heart.

The second deviation, with man putting himself at the
center of religion, is exemplified in this popular version of grace
before meals: "Bless us, O Lord; bless this meal and those who
have prepared it." We are actually asking God to bless the
steak ("this meal") and the cook ("those who have prepared
it")—which is perfectly legitimate, of course. But when Jesus
said grace, he gave thanks to the Father, the source of every
gift. Between both prayers lies a gaping gulf. A "Eucharistic"
prayer has deteriorated into an ordinary prayer of petition for
man; a theocentric religion ("Blessed be God!") has thinned
into an anthropocentric religion ("Bless us!"). This is symp-
tomatic of what happened to the offertory.

Where the first deviation sins by excess in regard to man's
offering, the second sins by defect. Since we cannot offer God
anything—outside of Christ—which is worthy of his glory, some
conclude that they need not offer him anything at all. This attitude launches a disintegrative process in which the sacrificial
meaning of the Eucharist is rapidly lost. A. Vergotte describes it
very well: "In order to evade the uneasiness created by the tran-
scendental conception of the Mass, people today tend to reduce
the Eucharist to two themes: spiritual nourishment and fellowship meal. Still, when isolated from sacrificial evolution, the

theme of spiritual nourishment seems in its turn to smack of magic, and that of the fellowship meal lapses into a purely horizontal symbolism."[19] In other words, when a community no longer celebrates Christ's sacrifice or enters into it, they end up assembling merely to eat together, among friends. Sometimes, finding there is no true fellowship of love on the community level, they even omit the fellowship meal, since it no longer expresses anything. Then the erosion of the community's sacrificial sense stops by itself, simply because there is no more community at all.

In the sacrifice of Christ

Let us try to understand correctly how the Church, without detracting from Christ's sacrifice, can pray to the Father:

From age to age you gather a people to yourself,
so that from east to west
a perfect offering may be made
to the glory of your name. . . .
May [the Spirit] make us an everlasting gift to you.[20]

The new covenant abolishes the sacrificial economy of the old, so that we need no longer offer lambs, bulls, wheaten flour or libations of wine. But it does not abolish the duty of love which they represented. Above all, it does not eliminate the weight of the cross each of us must bear if we would walk more joyfully toward heaven. Instead, it intensifies, by purifying it, the ascensional movement of our heart as we offer ourselves to God, together with our entire being and our most vibrant affections, so as to escape the despair of that prison which every human life is. This is how Paul describes the new spiritual worship, which is opposed to pagan worship and renews Jewish worship: "Think of God's mercy, my brothers, and worship

---

[19]A. Vergotte, "Dimensions anthropologiques de l'Eucharistie," in *L'Eucharistie, symbole et réalité* (Gembloux-Paris: Duculot-Lethielleux, 1970), pp. 35-36.

[20]Eucharistic Prayer III.

him, I beg you, in a way that is worthy of thinking beings, by offering your living bodies as a holy sacrifice, truly pleasing to God" (Romans 12:1).

Surely, such spiritual worship was already the ideal toward which all ancient sacrifices tended. But the new covenant added a particular richness to it: existential reference to the sacrifice of Jesus. We have no chance of being heard unless the Father recognizes his Son's voice in our prayer; there is no possibility that our holocaust will be accepted unless it is presented in Christ. Paul says very beautifully that we are "Christ's incense to God" (2 Corinthians 2:15) and that Christ gave himself up "as a fragrant offering and a sacrifice to God" (Ephesians 5:2). In a cogent paragraph, Vatican II urges the faithful, through the Eucharist, to graft their entire life onto Jesus' sacrifice:

> All their works, prayers, and apostolic endeavors, their ordinary married and family life, their daily labor, their mental and physical relaxation, if carried out in the Spirit, and even the hardships of life, if patiently borne—all of these become spiritual sacrifices acceptable to God through Jesus Christ (cf. 1 Peter 2:5). *During the celebration of the Eucharist, these sacrifices are most lovingly offered to the Father along with the Lord's body.* Thus, as worshipers whose every deed is holy, the laity consecrate the world itself to God.[21]

Let us note that this sacrifice of ours as Christians, insofar as we unite it with Christ's, is inscribed in the very account of the last supper. As a matter of fact, in the discourse after the institution as recorded in Luke 22:28-30, Jesus told his disciples:

> You are the men who have stood by me faithfully in my trials; and now I confer a kingdom on you, just as my Father conferred one on me; you will eat and drink at my table in my kingdom.

This statement ushers us into the life of the early community, which, as we know, encountered manifold opposition: per-

---

[21] *Dogmatic Constitution on the Church*, 34 (italics added).

secution by Judaizers, who considered Christianity a betrayal of
the ancient Jewish faith; and persecution by pagans, who saw
the Nazarene as the destroyer of their pantheon. Luke sums up
this difficult situation in a sentence that mingles hope with
sadness: "We all have to experience many hardships before we
enter the kingdom of God" (Acts 14:22). There were in the
community those who remained close to Jesus throughout such
ordeals; but there were also those who, like the seed sown on
rocky ground, lacked firm faith and gave up "in time of trial"
(Luke 8:13). Luke reminds us that sharing the Eucharistic meal
does not guarantee sharing the banquet in the kingdom. For
that, something more is needed: being constant amid afflictions
and standing faithfully by the Lord.

Christ's statement, furthermore, has a bearing on sacramental practice in today's Christian community. The Eucharistic ideal is, not sacramental overfeeding, but the living of the
Christian life. Every Eucharist is a promise to stand by Christ,
to hold fast with him in his trials. Far from celebrating a fervor
huddled over its own piety, far from shutting out daily reality
and contemplating the table of the kingdom in some glorious
beyond, every Eucharist takes a hard look at the world and its
suffering, and, with Christ, overcomes its tribulations.

The Mass at the heart of the world

In all things, Christ is the firstborn. His cross is the firstborn of all the crosses carried in the world. His tomb is the
cradle where all sacrifices are deposited for rebirth in his resurrection. As the sacramental actualization of Calvary, the Mass
is at the heart of the world.

Mankind's participation in the Lord's sacrifice—or, if you
will, the celebration of this universal Mass—takes place on different levels.

First, on an invisible and implicit level. Any man of good
will who offers his life for a cause he deems just, whether in the
single oblation of martyrdom or war or in the drop-by-drop
oblation of a lifetime dedicated to some absolute (which, ulti-
mately, is God), even if he does not know God's name, even if

he believes Jesus Christ is a hoax, even if he fights the Church in the very name of that ideal—that man, I say, is associated in the sacrifice of Christ. He is celebrating the Mass, though he may be lost deep in the Congolese bush, the steppes of Siberia or the gray anonymity of our modern cities; he takes part in the Eucharist even if he lived hundreds of thousands of years before Christ. For Christ is the firstborn of all creatures, and his cross is contemporaneous with all ages.

Secondly, on an implicit level, but in the knowledge of the faith. Every Christian who shares in Christ's life also carries Christ's oblativity within himself at each moment of his existence. Though Christ died "as a ransom for many" (Mark 10:45), this substitution was not meant to dispense us from bearing our portion of the world's sufferings and agony, but precisely to deepen our participation in his sacrifice and, therefore, in his resurrection. "Always, wherever we may be, we carry with us in our body the death of Jesus, so that the life of Jesus, too, may always be seen in our body" (2 Corinthians 4:10). Hence, every Christian life is a Mass in the world. Just as there is a proclamation of the Word of God at each Mass, so do the events of every day, mirrored in the Word, speak to us of God and show us his face. Just as there is also a consecration of the offering at each Mass, so do the bread of our deeds and the chalice of our joys and sorrows become "Eucharist," thanksgiving through Christ.

And, lastly, on an explicit and sacramental level, by participating in the Eucharist—especially through communion. This participation will be all the more authentic as it expresses the striving of an entire Christian life and positive concern for the joy and sorrow of mankind.

THE LANGUAGE OF SIGNS

The last supper was the prophetic enactment of Christ's death. This enactment was possible only because the signs used —the bread, the wine, the meal—were meaningful. The Mass is the memorial enactment of his death. In like manner, this memorial is possible—reasonably—only because the elements used, even when transubstantiated, retain their meaning.

The bread

The Israelites thought of bread as coming from the hands of God and reminded themselves of that by asking him for it every day (Matthew 6:11). It also represented their daily work, since they tore it from the earth with sweat on their brow (Genesis 3:19).

It was not only part of every meal but the main part. When Mark wants to show how the crowd kept milling about Jesus and his followers till they had no time for a meal, he writes, "They could not so much as eat bread" (3:20, Greek); and when a diner who has heard Jesus speak envisions the joyous feast in the kingdom, he cries out, "Happy the man who will eat bread in the kingdom of God!" (Luke 14:15, Greek).

Scripture mentions various types of bread: the bread of joy (Ecclesiastes 9:7), the bread of tears (Psalm 80:5), the bread of suffering (Isaiah 30:20), the bread with the taste of ashes (Psalm 102:10), the stale bread of idleness and the bitter bread of wickedness (Proverbs 4:17; 31:27).

In presenting the bread of the firstfruits (Leviticus 23:20), the Israelites wished to indicate that not only the first sheaf but the entire harvest belonged to God, not only the first loaf but the entire bread hutch was his. They received everything from his love, and they used to say (Psalm 145:15-16):

> Patiently all creatures look to you
> to feed them throughout the year;
> quick to satisfy every need,
> you feed them all with a generous hand.

The wine

The Bible speaks well of wine—one of those joys God

grants us during our life here below. In the words of Ecclesiasticus 31:27-28,

> Wine is life for man
>   if drunk in moderation.
> What is life worth without wine?
>   It was created to make men happy.
> Drunk at the right time and in the right amount,
>   wine makes for a glad heart and a cheerful mind.

Taken in moderation, it can be used as a remedy for sadness: "Procure strong drink for a man about to perish, wine for the heart that is full of bitterness: let him drink and forget his misfortune, and remember his misery no more!" (Proverbs 31:6-7). In Palestine, where people drank water at ordinary meals, wine betokened a feast—which shows that the Mass is not an ordinary meal, but indeed, as Paul says (1 Corinthians 11:20), "the Lord's supper." Jesus himself did not scorn the joy of wine, and the Pharisees, those gloomy abstainers, censured him for it (Matthew 11:19).

A symbol of friendship (Ecclesiasticus 9:10), of love (Song of Songs 1:4) and of the joy of living (Ecclesiastes 10:19), wine was an integral part of offerings (1 Samuel 1:24) and libations (Hosea 9:4). We read of Melchizedek, the priest-king of Salem (Jerusalem, no doubt), bringing bread and wine to Abraham, perhaps to celebrate a covenant meal with him (Genesis 14:18). Later, the Gibeonites also brought bread and wine to make a treaty with Joshua (Joshua 9:12-14). From the third century on, Christian tradition would view those offerings as a prefiguration of the Eucharist.

Thus, when the community presents the Eucharistized bread and wine to God, the symbolism of its offering is, first of all, cosmic. Creation—present in the bread and wine, "fruits of the earth"—is placed in God's hands, once it has become the body of Christ. The symbolism is also anthropological. Only man's ingenious labor can transform creation to produce that bread and wine; so his work and his whole life, too, are offered up and become the body of Christ. Lastly, the symbolism is historical. It recalls Melchizedek's offering, which heralded that of Jesus, high priest "of the order of Melchizedek" (Hebrews 7:18).

Offering

The more we love something, the emptier we feel when we offer it to God. (One has only to think of Abraham offering his son.) And sometimes the feeling is permanent—as in the case of a holocaust, where the victim is destroyed by fire. This emptiness which the act of offering scoops out in our heart is the place for God to come into. It is the hollow in the soul waiting for him. It is the breach through which he can enter into the fortress of our personality. It is the wound his presence can heal.

In each of our dealings with God, there is a twofold movement: our call and his reply. To lose our life is to save it in God; to shoulder our burden is to rest; to deprive ourselves through sacrifice is to enrich ourselves for eternal life. Similarly, the Word can speak only if received by our silence, for silence affirms that our own words are superfluous and so remain hushed before the Ineffable. In the sacrifice of the Mass, likewise, man deprives himself of a good—bread and wine—which belongs to him like part of his heart, so that God may fill it with his love. The community offers bread and wine, and God gives it his Son.

Eating together

In biblical lands, a meal signified mutual friendship presented to God in prayer (p. 36). This bond established by conviviality might extend all the way to a covenant. When Jacob struck a treaty with Laban, he offered a sacrifice and sealed their pact with a meal. Genesis 31:54 says, "He offered a sacrifice on the mountain and invited his brothers to the meal. They ate the meal, and passed the night on the mountain." Allies were "those who ate your bread" (Obadiah 7). This wealth of symbols provides the background for the paschal meal which Jesus, through the last supper, linked to his sacrificial death. As we have seen, his sacrifice transcends the categories of sacrifice. It is a holocaust if we consider the fullness and irrevocability of the gift, which passes beyond the frontiers of death; it is a sacrifice of reparation if we consider the blood "poured out for the forgiveness of sin"; and, lastly, it is a communion sacrifice if we consider the meal. Not just a sacrifice, and not just a meal; but a sacrificial meal. Here, however, the paschal lamb is Christ. Whereas of old the participants in a communion sacrifice attained to communion with God by eating part of the victim, the faithful in the new covenant receive it by partaking of the Eucharistic cup and bread. "The blessing-cup that we bless is a communion with the blood of Christ, and the bread that we break is a communion with the body of Christ. The fact that there is only one loaf means that, though there are many of us, we form a single body because we all have a share in this one loaf" (1 Corinthians 10:16-17).[22]

THE NUMBER AND FREQUENCY OF MASSES

Let us bring the question into sharp focus. I am not talking about the Masses a priest is obliged to celebrate in virtue of his ministry, but about those he celebrates every day, either for his personal devotion or for that of the community. Neither am I considering the problem of the strictly daily Mass: must one, for instance, celebrate every twenty-four, thirty-six or forty-eight hours? Instead, I am discussing the number and frequency of Masses in general.

Vatican II strongly urged priests to celebrate Mass every

---

[22]A gesture that signifies participation in the sacrifice is the offering of the bread and wine for the Eucharist. For convenience' sake, this offering was changed into a gift of money. (In the Middle Ages, Honoré d'Autun—in *Gemma Animae*, I, 35; Migne, *P. L.* 172, 555—noted that the hosts were made *in modum denarii:* "in the form of a penny.") Therefore, it is not a question of paying the priest for a Mass. In the Old Testament, when believers presented a lamb for sacrifice, they gave it to the priest, not that he might keep it for himself, but that he might offer it to God. The priest, nevertheless, received a portion of the victim—not from the offerers, but from God.

The stipend and the priest's subsistence are two different problems. Beyond a doubt, Paul proposed the ideal. Unwilling to be a burden on his communities, as was his right (cf. Matthew 10:10), he wanted to be able to say with pride, "You know for yourselves that the work I did earned enough to meet my needs and those of my companions" (Acts 20:34).

day.[23] In the past, permission to say several Masses a day—three on Christmas or All Souls' Day—was deemed a favor. (Pius XII, on the occasion of his golden anniversary in 1949, allowed bination, and anyone failing to exercise this privilege would have been suspected of spiritual tepidity.) We should note, however, that the Council's recommendation applies solely to priests of the Roman rite. The other rites (Catholic or Orthodox), as venerable as the Roman in their antiquity, have different procedures. Thus, Patriarch Athenagoras used to celebrate Mass only seven times a year, "according to the rules of the Church of Constantinople."[24] In the Roman rite itself, daily Mass did not become general practice until the nineteenth century.[25]

In order to answer our question, different factors must be weighed. Some pertain to Christian sensibility. I shall simply say that we must avoid jolting it and that desirable changes, if any, must be effected with charity and patience. The other factors pertain to theology and are the only ones to which I shall call attention here.

The Mass is a source of grace and sanctification. On God's part, this grace is offered in infinite measure; but, on ours, it is received according to the measure of our faith and love. The Mass, therefore, should be celebrated as often—and only as often—as there is an increase in our faith and love, those two hands with which we reach out to God. On the level of alimentary hygienics, there is no guarantee that the ideal is to have a big meal every day. On the level of spiritual hygienics, there is no guarantee that the ideal is to have a Eucharistic feast every day. Even in the things of God, there can be spiritual overwork!

The Mass is "the summit of the Christian life," "the source and the apex of the whole work of preaching the gospel."[26] It

---

[23]Decree on the Ministry and Life of Priests, 13.

[24]O. Clément, Dialogues avec le patriarche Athénagoras (Paris: Fayard, 1969), p. 111.

[25]See Karl Rahner and Angelus Häussling, The Celebration of the Eucharist (New York: Herder and Herder, 1968), p. 96, note 8.

[26]Decree on the Ministry and Life of Priests, 5; cf. Dogmatic Constitution on the Church, 11.

should, therefore, be celebrated as often—and only as often—as it expresses its own mystery to the world and to itself. But there is no guarantee that, amid unbelief and in mission districts, celebrating the Mass is the best way to present "the summit of Christian life." There is no guarantee that, amid the hunger which gnaws at certain countries of the Third World like a cancer, holding a cultual celebration is the most significant way to reveal the Church as a community of love and an epiphany of God's love for the world.

The Mass is the actualization of the Lord's sacrifice. It should, therefore, be celebrated as often—and only as often—as it expresses and fosters our existential participation in that sacrifice. But there is no guarantee that celebrating the Mass is the best way to show that we take up Christ's cross by helping our brother carry his and by sharing in the pain and agony of the world.

The Mass is a proclamation of the Word of the Lord "until he returns." It should, therefore, be celebrated as often—and only as often—as it effectively accomplishes this proclamation in the world and in the Christian community. Here again, one can envision and sometimes prefer other modes of proclamation, which may be more productive under certain circumstances.

It would be possible to continue this line of reasoning by itemizing the various riches we have discovered. My purpose is, not to disparage the Mass, but to make clear the exigencies placed on us by celebrating it and, at the same time, to show how they outweigh questions of number and frequency.

In conclusion, let me say that an intemporal, disincarnate theology, without a hold on Christian reality, would answer our question by saying that two Masses are worth more than one, that three are worth more than two, and so on. But a theology which takes into account not only the Mass, but also those who celebrate it, would be more circumspect. Though the practice of daily Mass cannot invoke any tradition in its favor, either in the Roman rite or in the others, we must not conclude that it is wrong. Neither must we conclude that it is good. It simply expresses the piety and the sensibility of an era. There are signs, however, that a change may even now be under way. After the intensive practice of daily Masses, "Eucharistic totalitarianism" is yielding to other forms of piety and other expressions of the Christian life. The "Lord's supper" is seen in closer relationship with the "Lord's day."[27] At any rate, the question is, not celebrating fewer Masses, but celebrating them better.

[27] 1 Corinthians 11:20; Revelation 1:10. See the testimony of Justin, p. 27.

V

The Eucharist as Real Presence

THE LESSON OF HISTORY

Like the question of sacrifice, that of the presence bears the scars of past controversies. To see just how much they have influenced our own understanding of the Eucharistic mystery and even the formulas we use to express it, we must make a rapid historical survey and, as it were, clean the canvas of time.

In the patristic age, the real presence was not the subject of great theological debates, as were the Trinity, Christology and grace, for example. It did not constitute a special chapter in theology, entitled "The Real Presence." Still less was it a problem, but simply a grace to be lived quietly. It was viewed as part of the unique mystery of Christ. Here is a testimony from Irenaeus of Lyons (d. 202?), which links creation, incarnation and redemption:

> The prepared cup and that which was made bread receive
> God's Word and become the Eucharist, the body of

Christ. . . . A shoot of a vine that is buried in the earth bears fruit in its proper season; a grain of wheat that falls to the ground and dissolves rises again, multiplied in form by the Spirit of God that embraces all things; then by the wisdom of God it becomes useful to men, and, receiving the Word of God, becomes the Eucharist, which is the body and blood of Christ. So too our bodies, fed by the Eucharist, although buried within the earth and crumbling within it, shall rise again in due season, since the Word of God will give them the grace of resurrection.

In the spirit of the *Didache*, patristic literature was particularly fond of underlining the symbolism of the Eucharist. Saint Cyprian (d. 258) explains, "When the Lord takes bread composed of many grains united together and calls it his body, he is signifying the union of our people which he was carrying in him. And when he takes wine drawn from numerous grapes and calls it his blood . . . he is likewise signifying our flock unified by the fusion of a whole multitude."[2] Such statements form part of the treasury of Eucharistic belief.

The problem began—and would recur throughout the course of tradition—when, instead of speaking about symbol *and* reality, some posed the dilemma: symbol *or* reality, figure *or* truth. This was the subject of the famous controversy between Paschasius Radbertus (d. about 856), the abbot of Corbie, who so stressed the identity of the Eucharistic body with the body born of Mary that he could no longer see the symbolic dimension of the sacrament, and Ratramnus (d. after 868), a monk of Corbie, who, through excessive spiritualism, propounded a purely symbolic and spiritual presence, the presence of the efficacy *(virtus)* of Christ's body and blood.

Two centuries later, the dispute flared up anew when Berengarius, a brilliant professor of theology in the episcopal school at Tours, accentuated Ratramnus' doctrine. Insufficiently rooted in patristic soil, he was unable to maintain both the reality of Christ's body in the Eucharist and the figure: for him

---

[1]*Against Heresies*, V, 2, 3, quoted in *The Fathers of the Primitive Church*, selected and translated by Herbert A. Musurillo (New York: Mentor-Omega Books, 1966), pp. 140-141.

[2]*Letter to Magnus*, 6.

only the "similitude," or the "figure," was present. These discussions enkindled a great bonfire of clerical polemics. For fear of the flames, which were not solely theological, Berengarius—already condemned by the Synods of Rome, Vercelli (1050) and Paris (1051), and by the Council of Tours (1054)—signed a profession of faith at the Lateran Synod (1059), under Nicholas II. In it he admitted: "After the consecration, the bread and wine on the altar are not only the sign *(sacramentum)* of our Lord Jesus Christ, but his true body and blood; they are touched and broken by the hands of priests and ground by the teeth of the faithful in perceptible manner *(sensualiter)*." These were manifestly excessive formulas, as we shall see, and Berengarius recanted as soon as he could. But at the Council of Rome (February 11, 1079), he was once again obliged to recant his recantation. He died at peace with the Church in 1088.

Such battles were invaluable, for they compelled the theologians to fashion formulas that might state the mystery in terms of their era. This was the work of summists like Hugh of Saint Victor (d. 1141) and Peter Lombard (d. 1160), of truly remarkable scholars like Alexander of Hales (d. 1245), Saint Bonaventure (d. 1274), Saint Albert the Great (d. 1280) and especially Saint Thomas Aquinas (d. 1274). Saint Thomas represents Scholasticism at its zenith. Drawing chiefly from Aristotelian philosophy, he formulated the Catholic doctrine on the Eucharist in terms which became classic. Through the Ecumenical Councils of the Lateran (1215), of Constance (1414-1418) and Florence (1439-1445), despite a roadside accident occasioned by John Wyclif (d. 1384), these elements arrived straight at the Council of Trent, presented on a golden platter carried by Aristotle.

Alongside erudite theology, there was popular piety—an immensely heavy treasure of tenderness in the heart of the people. The disputes in academe loosed a flood of Eucharistic devotions, and its waves sometimes carried, we must admit, the best and the worst. Blessed Juliana of Mont-Cornillon (1193-1258), a Belgian Augustinian who was favored with heavenly visions, worked for the institution of a special feast in honor of the Blessed Sacrament for the diocese of Liège, and her efforts were crowned with victory when Pope Urban IV extended Corpus

Christi to the universal Church on August 11, 1264, and Clement V (d. 1314) added the octave and the procession. With the beginning of the thirteenth century came the practice of elevating the host after the consecration; and, toward the end of the same century, the chalice. Marvelous things were sometimes said to happen at that moment: the host would become radiant like the sun, or an infant would appear in the hands of the priest. Anyone who gazed upon the elevation was preserved from sudden death that day, and his house and barn were protected from fire. Consequently, if the priest did not raise the host high enough, the more fervent groaned or shouted, "Higher! Higher!" There were also stories of hosts which had bled. Though Saint Thomas explained that such blood—if there was any!—was surely not Christ's,[3] these hosts were exposed for public veneration. Eventually, non-miraculous hosts were also exposed, and this practice, joined to that of the elevation, gave rise to our "Benedictions of the Most Blessed Sacrament." (The oldest monstrances date back to the thirteenth century.) I should also mention the multicelebration of private Masses by the same priest on the same day. Pope Leo III (d. 816) is reported to have said Mass seven times a day, and sometimes oftener. In the tenth century, bishops like Dunstan of Canterbury and Oswald of York had to set limits, not on piety, but on the quest for stipends, by permitting only three Masses a day. This hunger for ritualism played havoc with the symbolism of the altar. The old rule had been formulated by Ignatius of Antioch (d. about 110): "One is the Flesh of Our Lord Jesus Christ, and one the cup to unite us with His Blood, and *one altar*, just as there is one bishop."[4] The multiplicity of Masses entailed the multiplicity of altars; and since they could not all be placed in the center of the sanctuary, they were set up in side chapels, against a wall or a pillar, wherever there was room.

---

[3]Saint Thomas devotes a whole article, full of good sense and kindness, also, to exorcising belief in apparitions of blood or of an infant in the host. See *Summa Theologica*, Part III, ques. 76, art. 8.

[4]*To the Philadelphians*, 4; see also *To the Magnesians*, 7, 2, both in *The Epistles of St. Clement of Rome and St. Ignatius of Antioch* (Westminster: The Newman Press, 1961), pp. 86 and 71. This rule was observed in the West until the sixth century, and is still observed in the East.

This led to celebrating the Mass with one's back to the people, and to praying the canon in a whisper. Everything holds together. The multiplicity of Masses devaluated their significance: what had been the thanksgiving of the community was reduced to the rank of a pious exercise sometimes performed for love of money.

Lastly, I might mention certain practices which were inherited from the patristic age and sometimes survived until the Middle Ages: for example, placing a host in the mouth of the dead or on their breast as viaticum, or adding three particles from a consecrated host along with three grains of incense to the relics deposited in the "sepulcher" of the altar. This latter custom persisted until the sixteenth century.

God alone knows what intense love for the Eucharist these devotions—some of which still mark contemporary piety—were attempting to express. One cannot approve all of them. They were not errors of the heart, but awkwardness in manifesting its faith. But the fact remains that the practice itself should conduce to what Scripture calls "soundness of the faith" (Titus 1:13).

Now, that was the very purpose of the Council of Trent: to heal the faith, which was sick as a result of the Reformation. On October 11, 1551, the Council voted the following two canons:

> If any denies that in the sacrament of the most holy Eucharist there are truly, really, and substantially contained the body and blood together with the soul and divinity of our Lord Jesus Christ, and therefore the whole Christ, but shall say that He is in it as by a sign or figure, or force, let him be anathema.
>
> If anyone says that in the sacred and holy sacrament of the Eucharist there remains the substance of bread and wine together with the body and blood of our Lord Jesus Christ, and denies that wonderful and singular conversion of the whole substance of the bread into the body, and of the entire substance of the wine into the blood, the species of the bread and wine only remaining, a change which the Catholic Church most fittingly calls transubstantiation: let him be anathema.[5]

---

[5]Denzinger, *op. cit.*, Nos. 883 and 884, p. 270.

The teaching of Trent is articulated around two poles.

The first concerns what we call "the real presence." In negative terms, Trent's intransigence means at least this: anyone who maintains that the consecration changes nothing in the bread and wine, but only our attitude toward them, would be outside the Catholic faith. In positive terms: the whole Christ is present in actuality, not just in figure or by his spiritual efficacy. In the sentences "This *is* my body" and "I *am* the true vine," the verb *to be* does not cover the same reality. In the second, it indicates a sign, a figure, an efficacy; in the sentence of consecration, it affirms an identity between the signifier ("this," "this bread," "this wine") and the signified ("my body," "my blood"). Already in his day Theodore of Mopsuestia (d. 428) spoke as follows: "Christ did not say, 'This is the symbol of my body, this is the symbol of my blood,' but, 'This is my body, this is my blood.' In so doing, he teaches us that . . . [the bread and the wine] are transformed *(metaballesthai)* into his body and blood."[6]

The second pole concerns transubstantiation. In order to explain "that wonderful and singular conversion," the Council has recourse to the Aristotelian concepts of "substance" and "accident." Placed in the presence of the Eucharistic mystery, Aristotle stammered out what he could. Substance is "that which exists in itself and not in another, and which constitutes the support of all that exists in another." The predicamental accident is "that which does not exist in itself but in another." In the proposition "This bread is white," the substance (that which stands "underneath"—*sub-stare, hypo-stase*) is *that which* is white; and the accident is the *white* of that which is. In the Eucharistic conversion, "the substance," "the interior," "the intelligible" of the bread become Christ's body. But "the accidents," "the exterior," "the sensible" of the bread remain. And, what is more, they fully retain their vocation: for us who are necessarily bound to the sensible, they serve as anchorage for the divine Christ on our terrestrial earth, as the cleft through which the divine reality of the Eucharist—the body and blood of the risen Lord—enters into our sensible world.

---

[6]*Fragments on Matthew 26:26.*

In the mind of the Council Fathers, it seems, "transubstantiation" was to be simply another formulation of "the real presence," designed to guarantee its specificity. Luther, as a matter of fact, admitted Christ's presence in the sacrament—but only *in usu*: in communion at Mass. On the other hand, he condemned the practice of reserving the Eucharist and had taken exception to the very term *transubstantiation*. Hence, it was necessary to affirm the irreducible originality of Christ's presence in the sacrament. The Fathers used the philosophical language they had at their disposal. They did not intend to tie the dogma to one single formulation for subsequent centuries—much less, to canonize a philosophy. They were simply affirming that, on October 11, 1551, "the Catholic Church designates this Eucharistic conversion by the very fitting term *transubstantiation*."

In 1965, more than four centuries later, Paul VI would again use Trent's terminology in the encyclical *Mysterium fidei* and assert that it is adapted to our era. But, as we shall see later, this in no way dispenses the community from running the risk of searching for an even more suitable terminology.

THE GLORIFIED BODY OF THE RISEN CHRIST

Wholly occupied lighting up transubstantiation with Aristotle's candle, post-Tridentine theology had somewhat neglected the fact that the body present in the Eucharist is that of the risen Christ. The Council of Trent, as seen through its texts, had slipped into a certain theological dolefulness. At any rate, the Eucharist it proposes does not move in the joy of Easter morning. Rather, it bespeaks death, it represents the bloody sacrifice on Calvary, it immolates Christ mystically. All that is very good, but incomplete. In Scripture, the glory of the resurrection shines back upon Golgotha, so to speak, and transforms the cross of infamy into a throne of glory: "And when I am lifted up from the earth, I shall draw all men to myself," Jesus said (John 12:32). The famous fourteenth-century motet *Ave Verum*,[7] whose Gregorian melody is as tender as a lullaby for a

---

[7]It appears in a missal of Cluny dating from the second half of the fourteenth century. See E. Bertaud, "Dévotion eucharistique," in *Dictionnaire de spiritualité*, Vol. 4, col. 1630.

dead child, eloquently reflects this spirituality fascinated by
Good Friday: this body really suffered *(vere passum)*, it was
pierced by the lance *(perforatum)*, it was immolated on the
cross *(immolatum)*, and it will be our salvation at the hour of
our death *(mortis in examine)*. And the resurrection? Never a
word about it! Let me also mention—mere details, of course, but
so suggestive—that the Mass is celebrated facing a crucifix
(Benedict XIV even issued a constitution on this subject in
1746); and that the Christ shown there usually is not the Christ
of the old tradition—namely, the Lord of glory or Christ-the-
Priest in the majesty of his triumph—but, instead, the man
Jesus in the throes of agony. And some churches, with their
fourteen stations for the Way of the Cross, look much more like
mausoleums than roads to the resurrection. Pius XII echoes this
Tridentine spirituality when he writes: "The sacrifice of our Redeemer is shown forth in an admirable manner by external signs
which are the symbols of His death. . . . The eucharistic species under which He is present symbolize the actual separation
of His body and blood. . . . Jesus Christ is symbolically shown
by separate symbols to be in a state of victimhood."[8]

Surely, we need not agree with Pius' symbolic reading but
are free to believe that most people, on seeing bread and wine,
think rather of the joy of living and of sharing a meal together.
Vatican II, in any case, kept its distance with regard to Trent
and remembered to talk about the memorial of the resurrection.[9] Because the course of history does not stop, congealed, at
the gibbet of Good Friday, but, through the resurrection, opens
onto God's eternity, the body present in the sacrament is indeed
the glorified body of the risen Christ; and the table he spreads
for the beggars of his love is indeed, not the altar of the cross—
which was overturned for ever on Easter morning—but that of
the resurrection, the feast which lasts eternally. "The idea of the

---

[8]*Mediator Dei* (1947), 70 (New York: The America Press, 1948), pp. 38-39.
[9]*Constitution on the Sacred Liturgy*, 6 and 47; *Decree on the Bishops' Pastoral
Office in the Church*, 15. Out of concern for historical truth, one must observe
that Trent does not totally forget the resurrection, since, to promote Corpus
Christi and processions in honor of the Blessed Sacrament, it states that "the
victory and triumph of his death are again made present" in the Eucharist (a
text quoted in the *Constitution on the Sacred Liturgy*, 6). But the importance
given to the resurrection is one of the characteristics of contemporary theology.

eucharistic body," writes L. Cerfaux, "is linked with the notion
of the risen body."[10] That is precisely why tradition has associated the Eucharistic celebration, not with the day of Christ's
death, Friday, but with that of his resurrection, Sunday, "the
Lord's day."[11]

The presence of the resurrection at the heart of the Eucharist allows us to take a new look at the mystery. Transubstantiation is not merely the conversion of substance A into substance B, even though B enshrines the divinity, as in the days
when Christ walked along the roads of Galilee. Instead, it is the
passage of a terrestrial substance, bread, into a reality from
another world, that of the resurrection; a passage similar to the
one which the power of the Spirit will effect when he makes the
body of our own eternity rise from the dust of the tomb. As a
risen body, therefore, Christ is no longer subject to any spa-
tiality, temporality or other "earthly" determination. He is not
cramped within the substance of the bread, and we would do the
faith a disservice by imagining, as in the Middle Ages, that an
infant Jesus would be more comfortable in the host than an
adult Christ. Nor is he "the divine prisoner of the tabernacle,"
since we may put the sacred species under lock and key, but not
the risen Lord. Of course, he remains the same Jesus who was
born of the Virgin—with his particular tone of voice, so that
Mary of Magdala recognized him at the tomb; with his own
way of breaking bread, so that the disciples from Emmaus were
overcome with joy; with his own style of cooking sardines on
the embers, so that John cried out, "It is the Lord!" But his
glorious body passes like a dart of love through the stone sepulchre. Light as a thought penetrating to the heart, subtle as a
sunray streaming through a stained-glass window, he appears in
the room where the disciples had taken refuge behind locked
doors. In a word, this is indeed the Jesus of history, but transfigured by glory. He no longer belongs to the world of bread
and wine and meals, for these signs are now but the symbols of
his celestial presence.

---

[10]*Christ in the Theology of Saint Paul* (New York: Herder & Herder, 1959), p.
282.
[11]*Constitution on the Sacred Liturgy*, 106.

When, in 1 Corinthians 15:35-53, Paul discusses the resurrection of the body, his explanation ends abruptly at verse 42. How could it have been otherwise,[12] since the realities he tries to suggest (vv. 42-44) belong to a world that is "wholly other":

The thing that is sown is perishable
but what is raised is imperishable;
the thing that is sown is contemptible
but what is raised is glorious;
the thing that is sown is weak
but what is raised is powerful;
when it is sown it embodies the soul,
when it is raised it embodies the spirit.

This "spirit-informed" body is the spiritual body, inhabited by the *pneuma*, God's breath of life. It is not some immaterial, evanescent body, lacking consistency. As Paul reminds us, the body is not destroyed, but "transformed": "Our present perishable nature must put on imperishability and this mortal nature must put on immortality" (v. 53). Such is the transubstantiation which converts a bit of bread dust into the body of the risen Christ.

The Eucharist represents the future of the world. Sacramentally—and, therefore, partially but nonetheless really—it contains the firstfruits of creation resurrected in Christ. A bit of soil, a fragment of the world, a bite of bread become the risen Christ. We sow bread, "fruit of the earth," and it rises as a glorified body; we sow "the work of human hands" together with the joy of living, and it rises as a glorified body; we sow the happiness of sharing one and the same love at one and the same table, and it rises as a glorified body. This is no longer bread baked by men to nourish their daily joys and sorrows; nor is it manna to survive in the desert, though death must eventually come. What we have here is "the *true* bread . . . which comes down from heaven" (John 6:33) and gives life without death. In resurrecting his Son Jesus, the Father "put all things under his feet, and made him . . . the ruler of everything" (Ephesians 1:22). Since that resurrection, Christ's body touches the stars;

---

[12]Cf. *Pastoral Constitution on the Church in the Modern World*, 39.

and since the first supper, a bit of bread and wine become the center of the universe each day.

THE PRESENCE OF CHRIST

"Know that I am with you always; yes, to the end of time" (Matthew 28:20). That, according to Matthew, is the last sentence Christ spoke before leaving his followers. Affirming his definitive presence in the community of believers, this joyful promise dominates the mystery of the Church. Yet, especially since Berengarius, the theology of the real presence has crystallized around the Eucharist and, most often, in a polemic context. The resultant discussions, continuing unabated despite the definitions of the magisterium, have sometimes disfigured the beauty of the Church's face. In actual fact, we may hold that there is only one "real" presence and that it expresses itself in different ways. Hence, this threefold division:

—Christ's presence in the Church;

—his presence in the Word;

—and, lastly, his presence in the Eucharist.

To make a long story short, let me say that Catholic belief stressed mainly Christ's presence in the sacrament and sometimes showed a certain indifference toward the value of the Word; that Protestant belief stressed his presence in the Word and sometimes neglected his presence in the sacrament; and that Catholics and Protestants together gave little thought to his presence in the ecclesial community.

In no case is the presence in the Eucharist called "real" as if the other modes of presence were unreal. What we are discussing, rather, is a single "real presence" effected according to different modes.[13] In no case, either, if we want to keep a total vision of the Eucharist, should we separate these modes of presence. At any rate, they dedramatize and relativize, so to speak,

---

[13]See the instruction of May 25, 1967, *Eucharisticum mysterium*, 9: "This presence of Christ under the species is called 'real,' not in an exclusive sense, as if the other kinds of presence were not real, but 'par excellence.' " (Catholic press translation.)

the problem of the real presence in the Eucharist, as well as that of the "validity" of the ministries in the various Christian confessions. For each confession should strive, not to "possess" Christ in the Eucharistic real presence—we cannot possess Christ as we would a nicknack—but to come as close as possible to the fullness of the gospel, there where the Lord is.

Christ's presence in the Church

I am speaking here of Christ's presence[14] in the midst of the Church as an ecclesial community gathered in his name: "Where two or three meet in my name, I shall be there with them" (Matthew 18:20).

The Church makes the Eucharist

What is the specificity of Christ's presence in the Eucharist as compared with his presence in the Church? Both presences are real and spiritual. But his Eucharistic presence is, in addition, sacramental; it is realized in the bread and wine consecrated for the covenant meal. From another angle, his presence in the community is anterior to the Eucharist; for, if the sacrament is to be made, there must be a community that wishes to celebrate the Eucharist and has the power to do so in its minister. Vatican II brings out this anteriority when it says that "Christ is present . . . in the person of the minister"[15] and only then in the consecrated species. The view according to which Christ would be in heaven first, and would then come down on the altar in the transubstantiation of the bread and the wine, is false, because it short-circuits the essential element between heaven and the bread: the Church, the people of God. It is not

---

[14]Theology differentiates other modes of God's presence: the divine omnipresence, which is God's *common presence* in all things; his *special presence* in the souls of the just as object of their knowledge and love; and his *singular presence* in Christ, who is the only recipient of it.

[15]*Constitution on the Sacred Liturgy*, 7.

because the Church would be an orphan pining for the presence
of the Lord, that she celebrates the sacrament in order to make
him present. Rather, it is because she already possesses his presence through faith and love, that she has received this power to
make him present in the bread and the wine also. And the faithful receive in communion the Christ whom they already pos-
sessed in their hearts.

In the celebration of this presence, faith is essential.
"Doing what the Church does" is the buoy to which the priest
himself clings amid his own hesitations. Whatever the darkness
he experiences, he celebrates the sacrament validly, for this is
not the Mass of his weakness, but the Mass of the Church with
the whole wealth of her faith. Whatever his community, also—
even if reduced to the minimum: at least one server, say the
rubrics—it nonetheless represents the universal Church: "In
these communities, though frequently small and poor, or living
far from any other, Christ is present. By virtue of Him the one,
holy, catholic, and apostolic Church gathers together."[16] Con-
versely, a priest who does not want to unite his celebration with
"what the Church does" cannot confect the sacrament, even
though he has received the priestly power. So, a priest who
would go into a bakery to consecrate the bread on the shelves,
or who would say the covenant words as a sacrilegious farce
during a meal, would be consecrating strictly nothing, for he
would not be doing "what the Church does." By the same
token, a nonbeliever who would unwittingly eat consecrated
bread would not for all that be communicating, since it takes
the faith of the Church to discern the Lord's body.

Besides the anteriority of the Church with regard to the
Eucharist, there is also a relation of origin: that which unites the
signifier with the signified.

In truth, Christ is the sacrament of the Father, the visible
and efficacious sign of the peace and joy he wants for mankind.
In Christ's face we read the Father's tenderness toward the

---

[16]*Dogmatic Constitution on the Church*, 26; cf. *Constitution on the Sacred Liturgy*, 7: "Every liturgical celebration . . . is an action of Christ the priest and
of His Body the Church."

world: he loves us so much that he gives us this only Son (John 3:16).

As for the Church, she is the sacrament of Christ, "the universal sacrament of salvation."[17] Her whole vocation consists precisely in being aglow with beauty, unblemished and unwrinkled, so that the splendor of the Lord may show through on her face.

And, lastly, the Eucharist is the sacrament of the Church. It brings a fraternal community together around one and the same table to share one and the same love. Such is precisely its mystery: a communion of love in Christ.

What is the relation between the Church-as-sacrament and the Eucharist-as-sacrament? It is simple. The Church is not some eighth sacrament; but, like Christ and in his wake, she is the primordial sacrament (the *Ursakrament*) of salvation. She assumes the seven sacraments within herself and subordinates them to herself as secondary sacraments.

The Eucharist makes the Church

The Church makes the Eucharist. Inversely, one may say, the Eucharist makes the Church. As the body of Christ, its specific grace is to form that body in unity (cf. 1 Corinthians 10:17). Saint Augustine explains: "If you are the body and members of Christ, it is your mystery which is placed upon the Lord's table, it is your mystery which you receive. . . . Be what you see, and receive what you are."[18] And Vatican II: "In the sacrament of the Eucharistic bread the unity of all believers who form one body in Christ is both expressed and brought about."[19]

There is no need to belabor the point, so obvious is it and

---

[17]*Dogmatic Constitution on the Church*, 48; cf. 1; *Constitution on the Sacred Liturgy*, 26; *Decree on the Church's Missionary Activity*, 5.

[18]*Sermon 272*.

[19]*Dogmatic Constitution on the Church*, 3; cf. 11 and 16; *Constitution on the Sacred Liturgy*, 47; *Decree on Ecumenism*, 2 and 15; *Decree on the Bishops' Pastoral Office in the Church*, 15.

so universally acknowledged. But there are two remarks I would yet like to make.

The first concerns charity in unity. It is a grace of the Eucharist. It is also a duty: this sacrament is "a meal of brotherly solidarity."[20] A community which celebrates the Eucharist amid the mutual indifference of its members is a living lie. There is no use having a tabernacle full of hosts if hearts are not brimming with charity. And if the faithful receive communion at the same table without knowing and loving one another, they are seriously disfiguring the face of the Church. But it is so much easier to adore the real presence of Christ in the tabernacle than to venerate that same real presence in our neighbor's heart and surround it with love!

The second remark concerns Eucharistic hospitality within ecumenism. There is grave danger, as the official texts regularly remind us,[21] in practicing Eucharistic hospitality between Christian confessions which have not yet achieved unity of belief. For pretense in this domain would be worse than the frank avowal of differences in the matter of faith.

But one may also ask—since the Eucharist makes the Church—whether there is not greater danger still in never sharing the Eucharist even though we have not yet achieved perfect unity. For the Eucharist is also a prayer. "O sacrament of piety!" Saint Augustine exclaims. "O sign of unity! O bond of charity! Whoever wants to live knows where he may live and has something to live on. Let him come, let him believe! Let him be incorporated in order to be vivified!"[22] But how shall we be incorporated into a single body if we never share the bread of unity? How assert that the Eucharist makes the Church if we refuse to walk together along this road which surmounts the walls of separation and unites in Christ?

Naturally, there must be a minimum of common belief. On the other hand, there must also be a minimum of holiness; but if

---

[20] *Pastoral Constitution on the Church in the Modern World*, 38.

[21] See *Decree on Ecumenism*, 8, and the documents of the Secretariat for Promoting Christian Unity: the *Directory*, 38 and s.; the instruction of June 1, 1972; and the note of October 17, 1973.

[22] *Commentary on the Gospel of Saint John*, 26, 13.

we wait for all Christians to be completely holy before they receive together, they never will. Therefore, we may ask whether opening the doors of Eucharistic hospitality as often as possible is not closer to the gospel than keeping them shut. As to the minimum of belief to be set, it could be kept at the level required for salvation. Now, the minimal conditions stipulated by Scripture—therefore, in the judgment of the Spirit of God— are simple. It is said: "If your lips confess that Jesus is Lord and if you believe in your heart that God raised him from the dead, *then you will be saved*" (Romans 10:9). Clearly, the yoke of God's Word is lighter than that of the Christian Churches. Of course, no one should wish for passional extemporaneous "intercommunions," and the ministry of authority is now more difficult than ever. But neither should anyone, in the name of the gospel, impose upon his brothers the Scholastic terminology and Aristotelian philosophy which Christendom did very well without for over a thousand years. May the Spirit of Jesus hasten the hour of the ecumenical Eucharist!

Christ's presence in the Word

"[Christ] is present in his Word, since it is He Himself who speaks when the holy Scriptures are read in the church."[23] This is the third mode of Christ's "real" presence.

This presence is not bound up with the Eucharist as if Christ were present in the Word only when the community celebrates the Lord's supper. But we discover how real it is precisely when we compare, or relate, it to the Eucharist. There are two tables: that of the Eucharist and that of the Word. At the first, Christ is present under the species of the bread and the wine; at the second, he is present under the veil of the words. And the veneration due to the Word is the very one offered to the Eucharist. Vatican II makes this luminous statement on the subject:

> The Church has always venerated the divine Scriptures

---

[23]*Constitution on the Sacred Liturgy*, 7.

just as she venerates the body of the Lord, since from the table of both the Word of God and of the body of Christ she unceasingly receives and offers to the faithful the bread of life, especially in the sacred liturgy.[24]

The Word, then, is as "venerable" as Christ's Eucharistic body; and the table of the Word, like that of the altar, offers the one same Lord. We must admit that the Christian community tends to forget this truth which, nevertheless, forms part of its tradition. "You who attend the divine mysteries regularly," Origen (d. about 253) explains to his fellow Christians, "you know with what respectful care you guard the Lord's body when it is given to you, lest any crumb of it fall and part of the consecrated treasure be lost. For you would judge yourselves guilty—and, in that, you are correct—if a single speck of it were lost through your negligence. Now, if you rightly exercise so much caution for his body, why would you imagine that neglecting his Word deserves less punishment than neglecting his body?"[25]

Everyone knows that the liturgy loves to give outward expression to its inner veneration for the presence of Christ in the Word. In ages past, evangelaries[26] were very richly ornamented, with bindings overlaid with gold, silver or ivory: they were, so to speak, the tabernacle of the Word. In 1379, Charles V donated a tenth- or eleventh-century evangelary in gold, on which shone thirty-five sapphires, twenty-four rubies, thirty emeralds and one hundred and four pearls. In Byzantine churches, the evangelary was always the richest treasure. Though piety in our day certainly does not entail reproducing the lavishness of former times, we should at least imitate the spirit that inspired it. A priest who would pull some cheap memo-pad out of his pocket —as one does a handkerchief—and then proceed to read the gospel from it, would be symbolically affronting the dignity of the Word.

---

[24]*Dogmatic Constitution on Divine Revelation*, 21.

[25]*Homilies on Exodus*, 13, 3.

[26]*The evangelary, or evangelistary, was a liturgical book containing the four gospels. The book containing the epistles was called the epistolary. These separate volumes have now been replaced by the lectionary, which comprises all the readings used in the liturgy of the Word.*—Translator.

Contemporary piety exposes the Blessed Sacrament on the altar. But antiquity exposed the evangelary: only the evangelary and the body of Christ enjoyed that privilege, a custom the Greek Church has kept to this day. In councils like Ephesus in 431, the evangelary was placed on a throne to signify the presence of Christ presiding over his Church. And Vatican II magnificently restored this practice of enthroning the gospels.

Since the time of Berengarius and as a reaction against his error, the West has held processions of the Blessed Sacrament. More ancient, and widely practiced in the liturgies of East and West, is the procession of the evangelary, with candles and incense, before the proclamation of the gospel. In seventh-century Rome, this procession was accompanied by seven torches—the seven golden lampstands of the Book of Revelation (1:12)—and the singing of the *Trisagion*.[27] Liturgists used to explain, "The procession of the holy gospel moves forward; this is the power of Christ triumphing over death!" The new ritual of the Mass (94, 131) has retained an optional "mini-procession" before the gospel: the priest may carry the gospel book from its place on the altar over to the lectern as if to say, "The words I am about to proclaim are not mine, but Christ's. They come from the altar, which represents the Lord." As to the lectern, it is the official place for proclaiming the Word of God only—nothing else. Its dignity is like that of the altar. Suffice it to say there still remains a great deal to be done so that, in accord with the new ritual (272), the wretched reading desk installed as a lectern in the sanctuary may be "converted" into a place worthy of bearing witness to Christ's presence in his Word.

To be sure, ordinary liturgies—especially in private homes —can settle for less cultual perfection, for, fundamentally, the greatest veneration a community can offer the Word is to conform its life to it. Still, splendor seeks, in its own way, to highlight this "real presence." Just as the Eucharist was instituted, not to be kept in the tabernacle and venerated there by the faithful, but to be eaten at the covenant meal—*ut sumatur insti-*

---

[27]Reminiscent of the *Sanctus* in the Roman Mass, the *Trisagion* (literally, "Thrice Holy") is an Eastern rite chant consisting of an invocation to the holy, strong and immortal God.

tutum, says Trent—so the Word is proposed, not merely to be read from the lectionary as a pious exercise in preparation for communion, but to be lived as the community's encounter with Christ Jesus. The celebrating assembly must listen to Christ Jesus, who says to it as he once did to the Nazarenes, "This text is being fulfilled today even as you listen" (Luke 4:21). It must recognize itself in the responsorial psalm—glorious in the psalms of kingship, weeping in the psalms of lamentation, joyful in the hymns, and confident in the supplications. It must actualize this Word of God's in the homily, which is nothing but the amplification of the eternal Word in our day—its incarnation, so to speak, in the celebrating community; for each assembly must have its own personalized reading of the Word and experience the mystery of the gospel's contemporaneity with all times. Lastly, it must express its heart's desires before God in the general intercessions, which are not an omnium-gatherum litany but the community's personal response to the Word it has just celebrated. This is a vast program, and some communities have barely begun. Sometimes the problem is inertia, sometimes ecclesiastical coldness; but, as everyone knows, certain glaciers take more than one summer to melt . . .

This presence of Christ's, we said, parallels his presence in the Eucharist. Hence, the reference to two tables. We should, however, form a deeper idea of the link that unites Word and Eucharist. As we have seen, the Sinai covenant was concluded on the Word which had been proclaimed (p. 6). Now, the Mass is the celebration of the new covenant; and the Word announced there, is like the preaching of that covenant. God seems to be telling his people, "If you want to renew my covenant today, if you want to receive the bread and the wine as Eucharist, here is the contract I propose to your love." And the celebrating assembly, like the one on Sinai, must be ready to answer, "All that Yahweh has decreed—in the readings, the psalm and the gospel today—we will observe and obey." Only then will the priest be able to take the blessing-cup and say with Moses, "This is the blood of the covenant that Yahweh has made with you, *containing all these rules*" (Exodus 24:7-8). On Sinai, as at each Mass, the Word constitutes the covenant.

Consequently, there are not two parts to the Mass, with the liturgy of the Word serving as the preliminary condition of the Eucharistic liturgy. Rather, says Vatican II, both parts "are so closely connected with each other that they form but one single act of worship."[28] *And this "one single act of worship" is the celebration of the covenant.* The covenant begins, not at the specifically Eucharistic liturgy (the presentation of the offerings, or the preface), but at the first reading.

But the most compelling example of the union between Word and Eucharist is unquestionably the very account of the institution. On the one hand, there is the proclamation of the Word, which is not some magic formula to bring the real presence about, but the narrative of the last supper; and, on the other, the bread and the wine which are transubstantiated and proclaim the Lord's death until he returns. The Word creates the Eucharist, and the Eucharist in turn proclaims the Word.

THE PERMANENCE OF THE REAL PRESENCE

Historical overview

During the first centuries, the faithful could take the Eucharist home with them to communicate themselves, give it to the sick or absent (see p. 26), or even carry it along on a journey as a pledge of protection. Reserving the sacrament posed not a few problems. Hippolytus (215) diligently warns, "Everyone is to take care that no unbeliever, no mouse or other animal eats of the Eucharist, and that no particle of the Eucharist falls on the ground or is lost. For it is the body of the Lord that the faithful eat, and it is not to be treated carelessly."[29]

In the sixth century, there grew the practice of lighting a lamp before the Eucharist; and, in the ninth, Leo IV (d. 855) wrote that the Eucharist was kept on the altar. As everyone

---

[28]*Constitution on the Sacred Liturgy*, 56.

[29]*Apostolic Tradition*, 37, in Deiss, *Early Sources of the Liturgy*, p. 68.

knows, this latter custom perdured till Vatican II. The advantage of it was that it concretized the link between the real presence and the Lord's supper, the Eucharist and the altar. And the disadvantage was that it veiled the symbolism set in motion by the Mass. The very purpose of the Mass is to make Christ sacramentally present on the altar; but if he is already present in the tabernacle, this symbolism is obscured.[30]

The practices of Eucharistic veneration and adoration which developed over the centuries—such as Corpus Christi processions, exposition and benediction, and visits to the Blessed Sacrament—expressed the community's belief in the real presence even after Mass. For Saint Thomas, this belief seemed so evident that he saw no need of devoting an article of the *Summa* to it. He contented himself with formulating this golden rule of Eucharistic sacramentalism: "The body and the blood of Christ remain as long as the species of bread and wine remain" (Part III, ques. 77, art. 5).

With the Reformation, Luther and Calvin limited the real presence—in the sense in which they admitted it—to the time of the actual celebration of the Lord's supper. Against them the Council of Trent issued the following definition:

> If anyone says that after the completion of the consecration the body and blood of our Lord Jesus Christ are not in the marvelous sacrament of the Eucharist, but only in use, while it is taken *[in usu, dum sumitur]*, not however before or after, and that in the hosts or consecrated particles, which are reserved or remain after communion, the true body of the Lord does not remain: let him be anathma.[31]

In keeping with this definition, Trent then defended the legitimacy of Eucharistic worship as practiced by the Catholic

---

[30]That is why *Eucharisticum mysterium*, 55, recommends that the tabernacle not be kept on the altar where Mass is celebrated, so that "the Eucharistic presence of Christ, which is the fruit of the consecration and should be seen as such, should not be on the altar from the very beginning of Mass through the reservation of the sacred species in the tabernacle."

[31]Denzinger, *op. cit.*, No. 886, p. 270.

community and of reservation in the tabernacle, principally for communion to the sick.[32]

The bulk of this teaching was repeated by Paul VI in *Mysterium fidei* (September 3, 1965), and constitutes what he calls "a wonderful example of the stability of the Catholic faith"[33]— at least within Roman Catholicism, one should specify. For other rites, such as the Coptic, for example, do not reserve the Eucharist; yet no one would dare claim that that tradition is less venerable than ours: it is simply different. As for the Protestant positions, they vary according to denomination. The text published by the Groupe des Dombes in 1972 represents a milestone in ecumenical investigation between Catholics and Protestants.[34]

The presence as a relation

To understand Trent's teaching properly, we must not consider the real presence in isolation, as a marvel of faith subsisting for itself, but put it back in the total Eucharistic context.

The real presence is always a reference to the Eucharistic meal. In the words of Trent, the Eucharist "was instituted in order to be eaten." We cannot separate the words "This is my body" from the invitation "Take and eat!" The perdurance of the presence is understood as a function of this relation. The bread is consecrated for the meal, but the meal is not what consecrates the bread. The sole purpose of Christ's presence in the bread is his presence in our heart through the reception of the sacrament; but the fact of accepting or refusing the gift does not

---

[32]*Ibid.*, Nos. 888-889, p. 271.

[33]See *The Pope Speaks*, Vol. 10, No. 4, p. 323.

[34]See *Vers une même foi eucharistique?* (Taizé, 1972), especially pp. 21-23.—M. Thurian sums up his belief, within contemporary Protestantism, as follows: "After the Eucharistic celebration . . . the real relationship between Christ and the Eucharistic species which remain is a mystery that must be reverenced. . . . It is not up to us to declare whether the real presence perdures or disappears. There is a mystery here to be respected. . . . Negligence in this domain compromises faith in the real presence, whereas well-balanced respect is a sign one truly believes in the presence of Christ's body and blood" (*L'Eucharistie*, 1959, p. 272).

change the quality of it: even when refused, it always remains a gift offered, the body and blood of the Lord.

Perhaps it would be well to point out the ambiguity in our notion of presence. This notion attains its fullness, not when presence is perceived as a local proximity, but when it is lived as a relation of knowledge and love. Take a young lover dreaming of his beloved as he rides the subway during the evening rush hour: he is absent from all those with whom he is present in the crush of the same car, but his heart keeps him present to her from whom he is absent. We have all attended meetings where we were "physically present," as people say, while our heart wandered a hundred miles off. In the same manner, the reserved host engulfed in the vastness of a Moslem city, or in the wilds of mission territory, is a presence only for the Christians who venerate it as such. To them, it is not an object enclosed in a tabernacle, but a life they receive insofar as they enter into relationship with it. "When the faithful adore Christ present in the sacrament, they should remember that this presence derives from the sacrifice and is directed toward both sacramental and spiritual communion."[35]

The relation between real presence and communion may be more or less close. It is optimal when the believer receives at Mass.

It appears less evident, yet remains quite as real, when someone who always forms part of the community, but cannot approach the Eucharistic table now because of illness or suffering, receives communion as a prolongation of the celebrating assembly's communion and in perfect oneness with it. How extraordinarily splendid this can be when it is the husband or the wife who, at the communion rite during Mass, receives two hosts and leaves, accompanied by the prayers of the assembly, to carry the Lord to the sick spouse and communicate together! Surely, no one could fail to understand that such a communion, though outside the Mass, lies deep within the grace of the Mass; for, if husband and wife are united in one same love, it is precisely that they may give one another the Lord.

---

[35]*Eucharisticum mysterium*, 50.

Again, the relation between real presence and communion may be more or less remote when one receives outside the Mass. But it truly exists, even though it is implicit. An example may help. When a mother kneads and bakes bread for her household, she had the family meal in mind. Now, even if that bread is eaten outside mealtime, it keeps its full significance: it is the bread earned by the father's work and shaped by the mother's love—a sign of their nuptial community and of their love for their children. So, too, in the Eucharist: the bread over which the word of the covenant has been spoken remains for ever "the bread of heaven."

In certain extreme cases, the symbol may be very tenuous, while the reality of grace remains entire. When prisoners in concentration camps shared a fragment of a host or a tiny drop of wine, there was no question of a banquet savored in joy, as the liturgical formularies aver. It still remained a sign; and, however tenuous, it proved vast enough to signify their common destiny with Christ and their fellowship in suffering.

As long as the sign of bread lasts

So great is the sensibility of Christians to everything concerning the Eucharist that the same questions about the veneration due the consecrated species keep cropping up regularly: "What becomes of Christ's blood if a priest tips the chalice over on the altar? What should be done when particles break off from the host and fall to the floor?"

We must once again go back to that principle of Saint Thomas' which dominates sacramental theology: Christ is present as long as the species of the bread and the wine remain. If the consecrated wine permeates the altar cloth, we can no longer say, "This is wine to drink," and, therefore, Christ is no longer present. If the particles of the host are so small that we can no longer say, "This is bread," Christ is no longer present.

Someone will object, "These particles can be of various sizes. At what point do they cease being bread?" An excellent question. The scrupulous, however, can complicate it by taking

magnifying glasses to distinguish the "bread" in the crumbs—
and then the real presence would depend on the number of
diopters used! The sacrament, let us remember, is a sign, and
any judgment on the existence of the sign is made *humano
modo*—that is, according to the ordinary, everyday way of judg-
ing things. Ask a ten-year-old child, "Is this bread [to eat] and
wine [to drink]?" If he answers "Yes," then Christ is sacramentally present; if he answers "No," then the sign of the bread and
the wine has disappeared and Christ is not present. A.-M. Ro-
guet puts it well: "In the Eucharist, what we see with our eyes is
the sign of bread. That sign has to be true, not merely with an
apparent, phenomenal truth: that bread has to be seen immediately as true bread."[36] This is good sacramental sense.

Another question: "How long is Christ sacramentally present in us after communion?" In the past, people who had just
received were advised to recollect themselves for a while so as to
be alone with Christ and benefit from this special moment of
grace. Today, they are asked to sing with their mouth full on
their way back from communion. What is right? Some of the
old catechisms used to tell of a saint who sent two altar boys
with candles—as if in veneration of the real presence!—to es-
cort a communicant who had apparently cut his thanksgiving
too short. The story was clever, for it allowed one to conclude,
"My brothers [or my children], one must take one's time to
make a thanksgiving." No doubt, he was a great saint, but this
is not a good story. In point of fact, Christ is present sacramentally as long as the sign of bread lasts—no more, no less. As
soon as the bread is eaten, or again, as soon as there is no more
bread to be eaten, as soon as it becomes part of our gastric con-
tents, Christ is no longer sacramentally present. The communicant becomes neither ciborium nor tabernacle nor monstrance. But his dignity is infinitely greater than that of a
soulless object: he himself is wholly consecrated to Christ, he
becomes "the body of Christ" (1 Corinthians 10:17), the living
temple of his presence among men.

---

[36]"Purifications à la messe et désacralisation," in *La Maison-Dieu*, 103 (1970),
pp. 63-64.

Eucharistic worship

Everyone knows to what extent, in the Roman rite, the worship of the sacred species reserved in the tabernacle has developed: we have exposition, benediction, processions and Eucharistic congresses, not to mention private visits to the Blessed Sacrament. All these "pious and holy exercises," as *Eucharisticum mysterium* (58-67) calls them, are to be highly recommended in the very measure in which they manifest the soundness of Christian belief. In this connection, I would like to make a few remarks:

It is well to remember the reasons for reserving the Eucharist, and their respective importance. *Eucharisticum mysterium* (49) does this admirably: "The primary and original purpose of the reserving of the sacred species in church outside Mass is the administration of the viaticum. Secondary ends are the distribution of communion outside Mass and the adoration of our Lord Jesus Christ concealed beneath these same species."

It should be noted that these "exercises" developed in proportion as the ordinary celebration of the Mass had foundered in ritualism. The more ceremonious the Mass became, like the etiquette at the court of the Great King, the more popular piety sought to reestablish contact with God through personal adoration of the Blessed Sacrament. The less Eucharistic the Mass was, the more devotion turned to the secondary exercises, such as benediction, holy hours, processions, and so on. For when the people are fortunate enough to have a Mass of great liturgical density, regularly comprising a celebration of the Word together with a well-prepared homily and general intercessions that spring from the Word, and when they are given periods of silence during the penitential rite, after the homily and after communion, to foster their personal prayer—in a word, when Mass is celebrated with dignity and truth, as the thanksgiving of the entire community—then that community, I say, no longer feels the need of concluding it with benediction complete with "O Sacrament Most Holy" and "Down in Adoration Falling." Only when the congregation's Eucharistic piety is skimped by Masses without soul, rushed through at top speed and offering little more than a chance to communicate, will it seek to satisfy its hunger elsewhere and, sometimes, in any way. Then, benediction will occupy more room, on the affective level, than the Mass; private visits will seem more important than communal celebration; and the rosary recited before the Blessed Sacrament exposed will replace the evening office—which, according to Vatican II, is one of the poles of prayer as well as "a source of piety and nourishment for personal prayer."[37]

Since the thirteenth century, the Roman liturgy has specialized in benediction of the Blessed Sacrament. A romantic halo surrounds this exercise, and reams have been written about the host "so white and pure." But if we exposed a cob of consecrated bread and a carafe of consecrated wine, we would offend Christian sensibility (which has always been thin-skinned on this subject), though we would be closer to the symbolism of the Eucharist.

If exposition helps piety, if a community is affectively attached to it—I am thinking of certain communities which were founded to adore the Blessed Sacrament exposed and which consecrate an important part of their life to it—there is no cause to refuse them the "sign" of the Eucharistic bread. And, what is more, everyone, to be truly human, needs these moments of adoration, where the silence is filled with God's presence and produces self-knowledge. The world will consider it time wasted, but we consider it time fully saved because fully consecrated to God. These moments lost in the silence of God are the best in our life. But, I must immediately add, that does not require exposition of the Blessed Sacrament. In any case, we do not see Christ, but only the sign of bread; we cannot reach him with our eyes, any more than we touch his risen body when we receive the host in our hand or on our tongue; we are no closer to him because the tabernacle has been opened or the host exposed in a monstrance; and sometimes we would be better advised to seek his presence in our neighbor—most especially amid the misery in the world—and to practice charity, which is the sign of this sacrament. These are theological truisms. They also make good Christian sense.

---

[37]*Constitution on the Sacred Liturgy*, 89-90.

PRESENT-DAY INVESTIGATIONS

The purpose of theology is to demonstrate the credibility and harmony of the faith, and thus reveal the sovereign harmony of God. Of course, he remains the Transcendent One; yet his revelation does not crush our intellect under an unbearable weight but, rather, guides it gently toward joy in the truth.

Now, the Scholastic formulation of the real presence by transubstantiation no longer satisfies the modern mind. Instead of bringing the mystery closer and making it congenial, it creates additional difficulties: difficulties that stem, not from the belief itself—for the mystery remains entire, and every believing intellect must kneel before it in "the obedience of faith" (Romans 1:5)— but from its expression. The Scholastic thesis, with its academic vocabulary, seems like a medieval knight in full armor suddenly springing up in the midst of a Sunday congregation. Already strongly shaken by Kant's critique, the idea of a reality dwelling under *(sub-stare)* and outside the world of phenomena no longer fits our conception of matter at all. Rather, we think of matter as a collection of molecules, themselves composed of atoms comprising electrons, neutrons and protons; and, if we want to state our belief in language the man in the street can understand, we must stop talking about "substance" and "accident," for he never uses these words in their Scholastic sense.

This observation is not to be construed as a criticism of Trent. The Church used the philosophy she had at hand—which happened to be Aristotle's. Called to the Council's witness stand, he spoke as well as he could. The Church used his philosophy, since it was that of the times; but, in so doing, she did not intend to bind herself to it. Similarly, she used Romanesque and then Gothic churches for her liturgy, not because Romanesque was better than Gothic or vice versa, but simply because each was the style of the period in question.

That we are therefore seeking a better way of expressing the mystery for our times testifies to a sound faith and a living piety. Of course, the mystery itself remains as immutable as God's eternity, identically the same the day Jesus instituted it and the day he returns to judge us. It overrides the constant changes of history. But we who speak use the changing words of a living language (only dead languages stay put). And the Church has not been empowered, in the name of the gospel, to twist the meaning of words for her own convenience or to radio-control philosophies as she chooses. It is only normal that she should defend her dogmatic formulations on the Eucharist by stating that they "are adapted to all men of all times and all places."[38] That is quite fair, as anyone would admit. But Christ did not equip her to prophesy that, in a century from now, people will still be giving a certain word—*substance*, for example— the same meaning it has today. She can create her own vocabulary for private use—"the tribal tongue," as it were; but, if she wants to speak to the world, she must use the changing language of that world.[39]

Transfinalization and transignification

The terms *transfinalization* or *transignification*, applied to the Eucharist, denote the fact of giving the consecrated bread and wine a finality or significance which *trans*cends their ordinary finality or significance. Some authors use these terms interchangeably, while others carefully discriminate between them. In any event, a transignification has value only if the new signification given is the highest, the ultimate—in other words, a transfinalization.

The starting point is this: the ultimate reality of things is, not their sensible or scientific or commercial value, but their

---

[38]*Mysterium fidei*, 24, in *The Pope Speaks*, Vol. 10, No. 4, p. 314.
[39]The possibilities in such investigations are limited. As the Dutch bishops declared on April 27, 1967, "We believe that investigation into the way Christ is present in the Eucharist can be left to the free discussion of the theologians, provided they firmly maintain that the bread and wine are changed into the body and blood of the Lord and that he is truly present under the Eucharistic species."—On the history of these investigations, which were influenced first of all by the works of J. de Baciocchi (1951), see E. Schillebeeckx, *The Eucharist* (New York: Sheed and Ward, 1968), p. 107 and ff.; and V. Warnach, "Symbol and Reality in the Eucharist," in *Concilium*, Vol. 40: *The Breaking of Bread* (New York: Paulist Press, 1969), pp. 82-105.

significance on the noetic or intelligible level—last of all, the significance given them by us or by Christ. Thus, a ring may take on diverse meanings. It may serve as a band for a carrier pigeon or, in some countries, be worn as an ornament for nose or ear. But what depths of love it signifies when exchanged as a nuptial covenant between spouses! And in this last case, its significance varies further according to circumstances. An engagement ring is filled with dreams of a lifetime of love and joy together; and the ring a widow wears in the evening of life, when she has garnered the last sheaves of her love, is a hope of seeing her husband again. Therefore, what counts in this ring, more than everything on earth, is not its chemical composition, its resistivity, its conductivity or any other of its "accidents," but, rather, the significance a life of love gives it. With regard to another ring, similar to it in every respect, this one has truly changed meaning—or, if you wish, its meaning has been transubstantiated: it has received a new significance, a transignification. E. Schillebeeckx offers another example: "A coloured cloth is purely decorative, but if a government decides to raise it to the level of a national flag, then the same cloth is really and objectively no longer the same. Physically, nothing has changed, but its being is essentially changed. Indeed, a new meaning of this kind is more real and more profound than a physical or chemical change. In the case of the Eucharist, too, a new meaning is given to the bread and wine, not by any man, but by the Son of God."[40]

What is this new meaning, this transignification? It is Christ's changing the gift of bread and wine into the gift of his body. This is the banquet of the risen Lord with his followers. And just as the bread and wine shared at a meal do not have a purely nutritional function or *finality*, just as their *significance* is not merely their caloric value but the expression of shared love, so the Eucharistized bread and wine are *transfinalized, transignified*: they are identified with the gift of Christ's body. Not the gift of the body, period, but of that body as the sacrament of the whole of salvation history: the body racked during

---

[40]*The Eucharist*, p. 113.

the passion, the body transfigured by the glory of the resurrection, the body sitting at the right hand of the Father to intercede for us till the end of time—in a word, the body which is the anamnesis of salvation.

Transfinalization and transignification do not replace the reality expressed by Christ's sacramental presence in the bread and wine. For the gift of self through the sharing of a meal remains in the order of intentionality. It is a symbol. So, too, the offering of a wedding ring does not realize the nuptial gift, but merely signifies it. Christ has to be present in the Eucharistized bread and wine for the gift of the bread and wine to become the gift of Christ.

What advantages are there to this new presentation of the Eucharist?

Trent's doctrine on the real presence ended in extreme reification. Instead of contemplating Christ seated at the right hand of the Father, many imagined him entering the bread as one enters a house, and then shutting himself up in the tabernacle. They were thus led to localize and materialize him in the "accidents" of the bread. The very word *transubstantiation* expressed this real presence in terms of things. Here, we prefer to express the mystery in terms of persons. Indeed, according to existential phenomenology, the presence of a person is not realized solely by the fact of being in-oneself or for-oneself, but essentially by the fact of being for-others. In the Eucharist, this presence is not willed for itself, but primarily for the faithful. Always offered, it attains its fullness when it is accepted. It functions on the level of interpersonality. There is a real presence in the host, assuredly, but it is secondary to that of Christ-Eucharist in the hearts of the faithful. The Eucharist was instituted, not to be kept and adored in the tabernacle, but to be received as a gift in which Christ places himself. Accordingly, we put less emphasis on the mode of the real presence and more on its purpose, less on the how and more on the why: an interpersonal meeting with the Lord.

In present-day discussions on the Eucharistic mystery, therefore, we can dispense with the vocabulary of Scholasticism and feel no regret. On the one hand, we need only underscore the symbolism and the grace of the Eucharist. On the other, we can express the real presence by returning very simply to the language of Scripture and the Fathers. To disquisitions in the idiom of Aristotelian philosophy, and even of Saint Thomas, we should prefer the clear and uncomplicated statement of Jesus: "I am the living bread which has come down from heaven. Anyone who eats this bread will live forever" (John 6:51).

The sacramental meaning of the universe

The world has a "sacramental" meaning. Every creature is a bearer of God's salvation and a revelation of his love. We dwell, as invited guests, in the vast palace of creation, where everything cries, "Glory!" (Psalm 29:9). Already, the bread of earth holds a foretaste of the bread of heaven, human joy is a door open onto the happiness of God, meals shared together are not unrelated to the banquet in the kingdom, and the love of a man for a woman is a road to the love of God. Sin would be mistaking the sign for the reality, stopping in midcourse instead of running toward the goal. Grace is discovering the reality through the sign, reading the Creator's name in his creation, and using the crutches along the way to find repose in God. In this manner, all creatures can receive a "transignification"—not that some new signification or finalization is arbitrarily added to their fundamental meaning, but that their own ultimate significance and finality are thereby set in motion. Now, in this symbolic line, the Eucharist stands at the summit of creation; for, in the Eucharist, the signifier (the bread given by God) is one with the signified (God giving the bread). It is the real presence of Christ at the heart of creation, its crowning by him who is "the Beginning" and who "holds all things in unity" (Colossians 1:17-18)—not so much the risen Lord's presence in a piece of bread as that bread's belonging to the sphere of the risen Lord. Indeed, just as we cannot say that the world contains God —not even when Christ becomes incarnate in the womb of a Virgin—but, rather, that the divine immensity contains the world; and just as we cannot say that God's eternity is situated

behind history—any more than before it—but that it encom-
passes time in its infinitude; so neither can we say that the bread
"contains" Christ, but, rather, that Christ assumes a little bread
and wine in his divine person and then transfigures the sons of
Adam who receive this bread into sons of God. Younger than
the world, the Eucharist places the world in God's eternity.

Thus, the universe does not live in anguished expectation of
disintegrating amid apocalyptic convulsions but, rather, in the
hope of participating in the resurrection of the Lord. All created
beauty preludes the resurrection. On the Christian level, it is important that a flower be garbed in bright-colored robes (more
beautiful than Solomon's!), that a bird sing as if to celebrate the
heavenly Father who feeds it, that a young girl be clothed in
grace as is Christ's bride, the Church. Does not all splendor,
even the humblest, announce the infinite splendor of the risen
Lord? Suffering and death itself take on a look of hope, because
in the Eucharist they can read their role in the resurrection.
Blessed be the day when God transfigures the whole of creation
into a Eucharist! Blessed be the day when there is no more "real
presence" in the sacrament, since God is "all in all" (1 Corinthians 15:28); when there is only one bread, that of eternal joy;
and only one feast, that of the kingdom!

VI

The Eucharist Today

The Constitution on the Sacred Liturgy was promulgated in September, 1963. Since then, what a marvellous way we have come! Those who worked to reform the liturgy long before Vatican II, those who fought with all their faith, accepting blows (there is no victory, even in liturgical matters, without battle; there is no battle without blows!), obtained nearly all they asked. But as soon as the authorities on liturgy proposed solutions, newer and more urgent problems arose.

The Church is Christ's fiancée. She is like a girl for whom a wedding dress is prepared with such great care and over such a long period that, when the dress is ready, she has outgrown it! But can we complain because a girl grows? That is her life! Can we complain because the Church embellishes herself? That is her grace!

How, then, can we measure our liturgical progress? It is vain to draw up balance sheets for today that will be meaningless tomorrow.

137

But it is worth illustrating the effect of Eucharistic theology on today's Christian life and on liturgical celebration. In order to do so, I here present, by way of conclusion, a few reflections of Theophilus as he attends a Sunday Mass celebrated by Father Elias. I would ask the reader's permission to use a literary genre—fiction—which was highly esteemed in Christian antiquity, since an apparently simple parable can often convey very serious teaching. (*Theophilus*, it will be remembered, was the name of the person, real or fictitious, to whom Luke addressed his Gospel.)

The numbers in parentheses refer to the pages on which these reflections are based.

TOWARD THE FEAST OF THE RESURRECTION

As Theophilus walks into church this fine Sunday morning, he can see signs of joy everywhere.

The altar—the only one in the church (p. 107)—manifests the presence of Christ gathering the community together. The twelve candles in front of the crosses of consecration have been lit, for, as the pastor, Father Elias, often says, "The Church is built on the foundation of the twelve apostles." On the other hand, he removed the fourteen stations of the Way of the Cross, which used to make the building look like a funeral parlor. On the cross in the sanctuary, a Christ radiating paschal joy seems to draw everything to him.

The music began long before the start of Mass. I must say the organist, Ms. Harmony, possesses the gift of creating an atmosphere of joyful welcome. Everyone keenly senses that the Eucharist is the feast of the risen Christ (p. 60), a weekly passover. Tirelessly, Father Elias repeats, "The church of stone must give witness to the church of the faithful, and express its mystery. It is a *Eucharistic* community, an assembly of praise and thanksgiving, celebrating the resurrection of Christ. If not, then the church of stone unceasingly destroys the mystery created by the liturgical celebration. So many churches of stone, instead of gathering the people, disperse them in the pews!"

Theophilus is always very happy to see the welcoming committee waiting for him. "At Mass," Father Elias reminds everyone, "we form a family. The Eucharistic Prayers say so, explicitly. Let's not make the liturgy lie." Then he adds, " 'God does not make his home in shrines made by human hands' [Acts 17:24], but in the heart of those who gather together in his name" (p. 115). He also wants each individual to feel comfortable as if he were in his own home, and loved as if he were the only person present. "What good would it do to have a tabernacle full of hosts if our hearts were empty of brotherly love?" One day, he quoted to the parish council an ancient, third-century text in which the bishop was told, "If a poor man or a poor woman comes, whether they are from your own parish or from another, above all if they are advanced in years, and if there is no room for them, make a place for them, O bishop, with all your heart, even if you yourself have to sit on the ground."[1] To tell the truth, the situation had not yet arisen in Theophilus' parish, but everyone smiled at the thought of the bishop sitting on the floor. At any rate, they understood that sharing the Eucharistic bread obliged them to shower loving attention on the lowliest.

Our Lady

Theophilus greets with a smile of veneration and tenderness the very beautiful statue of our Lady. Simple as a little girl, refined as a princess, tender as a mother, she wears an expression of glory this morning—the same expression she wore, he supposes, on the morning of her Assumption. "Just right," he thinks, "because, as the Council said, the saints especially express the paschal mystery of the Lord."

The "Paradise" of the saints

In the past there was in the church a whole litany of other

---

[1]*The Didascalia of the Apostles*, 12, in L. Deiss, *Early Sources of the Liturgy*, p. 91.

statues of holy men and women in plaster. Now, Father Elias
has always revered the saints and the angels, but he has little
veneration for plaster. So he gathered all the statues, with their
individual money boxes, into a side chapel which he baptized
"Paradise." Here each person can seek and find his or her saint
and offer devotion as well as money, because it is his principle
never to take something away without proposing something new
and better. As he says often, "We must not shake the grandmothers!" And he adds, "The grandmothers are often not the
ones you think. Some young people, at twenty or thirty, already
have the souls of antiquarians!"

Chapel of the Blessed Sacrament

As Theophilus passes the chapel of the Blessed Sacrament,
he pauses for a moment to venerate the Lord present in the
Eucharist. He has noticed how the chapel is always tastefully
decorated, even during the penitential seasons of Advent and
Lent. It is always so inviting that one feels like stopping for a
while. That is where the sacred species are reserved as communion for the sick (p. 129).

A Celebrating Heart

Well before the community begins to sing "This is the day
the Lord has made," Theophilus' heart is already in a festive
mood. This morning, while setting his necktie out for him, Philothea, his wife, urged, "Here, wear your 'festive' tie—the one
you like." He agreed, for every Mass should be a feast. As for
her, she is wearing the pendant he bought her for their wedding
anniversary: a lovely little gem—nothing costly, but quite at-
tractive on her. She explained, "Beautiful things remind me of
the risen Christ (p. 136). So I'm wearing this today." Darling
Philothea! She can always find a reason to wear her pendant;
but, for once, this liturgical motive was valid.

THE CELEBRATION OF CHRIST PRESENT
IN THE WORD

It is already time for the first reading. Whenever the Word
of God is proclaimed, Theophilus is overwhelmed by holy respect, as before the real presence of Christ in the Eucharist. He
empties his heart to fill it with the presence of God. "How wonderful!" he reflects; "God still speaks to each of us today, and
we can each experience how contemporary the Word is!" As
Father Elias has taught them, "The Eucharist begins with the
first reading; the Word of God is like the preaching of the covenant. If you want to partake of the covenant meal, if you want
to receive Christ's body and blood, you must first say 'Yes' to
the Word God speaks to you today" (p. 122).

Philothea steps up to the pulpit for the reading. She was
chosen for this ministry, not because she serves on the liturgical
committee, and still less because she is personable ("That she
is!" nods Theophilus), but simply because she is a teacher of
diction. Father Elias, you see, explained that the idea is, not to
give everyone a try at reading, but to ensure an intelligible
proclamation—something worthy of Jesus: "In the Church,
everyone should exercise his particular charism: those who sing
well should sing, those who paint well should paint, those who
read well should read, and those who dance well should dance."
Theophilus cannot believe that some parishes pick readers at
random and give them no time to prepare. In his words, "Naturally, everyone knows how to read. But mere reading is not
the point. The reading should be an effective proclamation of
the Word of God. Even more than that, it should put before the
community Jesus Christ, who is present in his Word, for he it is
who speaks when the holy Scriptures are read in the Church."[2]

Philothea proclaims the sacred text with infinite dignity
and simplicity. Her voice penetrates through the assembly as if
to engrave the words in everyone's heart of hearts. The pulpit is
placed in what we might call the affective center of the assembly, exactly where Jesus would stand if he came to speak in per-

---

[2]*De Sacra Liturgia*, 7.

son. Father Elias wants it to be according to the rubrics: "the suitable place demanded by the dignity of the Word of God, a fixed pulpit and not a simple moveable stand."[3] And only the Word of God is proclaimed there. The pulpit is a dignified place for the Word, not the place for words! "Why are there still so many churches," Father asks himself, "which do not yet know or fulfill these wise decisions of the new *Order of the Mass*?" He also likes to explain—but this is his personal liturgical feeling—"There must not be any dead space between the Word and the assembly. In ancient Syrian churches, the pulpit was right in the middle of the faithful." To listen to the reading, Elias himself sits, not facing the community, but with it. He has long since relegated to the cellar the throne of yesteryear, from which he used to dominate over the people like a satrap holding forth on a dais. "To preside," he insists, "is not to dominate, but to render a hierarchical service. In the school of Christ, we are all fellow students. And if the priest has a priority, it's to listen to the Word with greater humility and practice it with greater truth!"

The gospel procession

How beautiful the gospel procession[4] is today! From the beginning of the Mass, the gospel book has been set upright on the altar.[5] Mr. Page, a retired bookbinder, has bound it to perfection and placed on the cover an icon of Christ. When you enter the church, Christ on the altar seems to welcome you (p. 121). As for the pulpit, it is in the same style and of the same material as the altar, so that everyone can plainly see there are two tables—that of the Word and that of the Eucharist (p. 119). Father Elias takes the gospel book from the altar, the table of the Eucharist, and carries it in procession to the lectern, the table of the Word, accompanied by candles which Mr. and Mrs.

---

[3]*Order of the Mass*, 272.
[4]*Order of the Mass*, 94.
[5]*Order of the Mass*, 84.

Durand hold, while their twin daughters—fine girls of eighteen
—carry roses: the whole family surrounding Christ the Word as
with a crown of beauty. Elias often says, "In the liturgy, we
need not just clear ideas, well-constructed homilies and well-ex-
ecuted rites, but beauty, too, and splendor and harmony!" And
sometimes he exclaims, " 'Long live Yahweh, whom I serve!'
[This prayer from the prophet Elias, in 1 Kings 18:15, has become his cry of joy, you might say.] All earthly beauty is the
face of Jesus among us! And we have to transform our human
joy into Eucharist, into the Lord's body!"

The homily—Word of God

Father Elias wants his homily to be nothing but the actualization of the Word on the level of his community (p. 122):
"What I try to give you is, not my own words, but God's. And
on judgment day, may Jesus recognize as his own all the words
I have spoken!" But Philothea feels—and, quite likely, her feminine intuition is correct—that God shows through most in the
homilies when Father is most personally involved in what he is
saying: as if he were tearing out pieces from his own heart.
Theophilus, for his part, often dwells on Paul's words to the
Thessalonians: "You accepted [the Word] for what it really is,
God's message, and not some human thinking" (1 Thessalonians 2:13).

"Speak, Lord; your servant is listening"

To tell the truth, this morning Father Elias' homily is not
getting off the ground. It was well prepared (in consultation
with the liturgy team), but, as he well knows, some days homilies fall flat. A good homily is a gift of the Lord. Father Elias
concludes his homily today, as he often does, "If you find that
my homily is not too good, I leave you a few moments of
silence during which the Spirit may continue to give a better one
within your heart." No priest can take God's place in this ir-

replaceable homily, this intimate talk to Theophilus. In the conscience of every human being there is a threshold which none
can step across, the point at which men's words die out and the
murmur of the Spirit begins. Behind this threshold, Theophilus
is totally in his own domain, like a king. Then, in the royal au-
tonomy of his conscience, he can say humbly, "Speak, Lord;
your servant is listening!" (1 Samuel 3:11).

Theophilus has heard that, in a neighboring parish, they
sometimes read newspaper clippings instead of the Word of
God—to be "relevant," as they say, to be "with it" and "where
it's at." This horrifies him, for he realizes that, in the Eucharist,
the covenant is built on the Word of God, not on that of a
newspaper. Of course, Elias himself often quotes news items
and secular literature in his homily—but always to illustrate the
Word, never to replace it. He knows that the most biblical of
homilies, the one closest to God, is the one that brings God's
Word closest to man—necessarily, for there is no one more
human than God.

Charity—the first liturgical rule

When Theophilus hears of practices which he does not approve, he is careful not to pass judgment on them. "Perhaps,"
he says to himself (although he hardly believes what he is saying), "this parish has received a special permission from the
Pope." He prefers to be wrong through a false judgment rather
than uncharitable through a rash one. He reminds himself that
Father Elias often says with enthusiasm, "The first rule in liturgy and the first of all rubrics is brotherly love."

The organ

Ms. Harmony is surpassing herself today in her organ
playing, creating an atmosphere of meditation after the homily,
playing the Bach chorale *Ich ruf zu dir, Herr Jesu Christ.* The
chorale melody, played on a trumpet stop, rises in the silence of
the assembly, supported by a bourdon accompaniment like the

beating of a heart. Ms. Harmony has the gift of making notes weep, chords laugh and rhythms dance exactly when they should and as they should. What Theophilus remembers reading somewhere is true: to have a good organist for the Eucharist is a gift of the Lord.

The general intercessions

It is the Schneiders' turn to do the honors this morning. The liturgy team has decided that each Sunday some family will take over this ministry. So far there has been no shortage of volunteers. The Schneiders are not intellectuals ravaged by metaphysical anxiety, and their prayer intentions have no literary varnish. But their words do hit the bull's-eye: they land like harpoons in the hearts of the faithful, drawing all to prayer.

All the petitions are rooted in the Word of God. There are none of those pass-key formulas that might be offered anywhere (which also means nowhere). They are the words of the assembly responding prayerfully to the Word of God. Father Elias has explained: "If you don't want the general intercessions to be a duplication of the liturgical litany which follows the consecration, you must constantly come back to the Word of God. The intentions should rise from the scriptural meadow like crocuses appearing in the fields of spring. And make sure that the petitions are universal. This is the way our assembly shares the burden of human pain. The Mass is the prayer of the entire Church for the entire Church!" However, that does not prevent the community from adding its own intentions, once the Schneiders have finished reading their text alternately.

CELEBRATION OF CHRIST PRESENT
IN THE EUCHARIST

The problem of the offertory—I should say the presentation of the offerings—was resolved long ago. In the new ritual there is no offertory, but rather the "preparation of the altar and the gifts." Father Elias believes that symbolism should be respected. The bread should look like bread (not like white cardboard which does not express the "sign" of bread), and the chalice should look like a cup of wine (p. 96).

The procession of the gifts

Each Sunday this expressive "ministry," the carrying of the offerings to the altar, is entrusted to one family. The community takes the instruction in the new *Order of the Mass* very seriously: "It is fitting that the participation of the faithful be expressed by their offering the bread and the wine for the celebration of the Eucharist."[6] At every Mass, even weekday Masses, there is always a procession of the gifts.

The altar—sign of Christ

The sanctuary has been furnished in good taste. At the suggestion of the National Committee for Religious Art, the altar (p. 107) has been reduced to more reasonable dimensions: a cube of about three feet on each side. With use, it seems to have acquired more presence. Its dignity has been accentuated with the processional cross and a seven-branched candelabrum as beautiful as a tree bearing fruits of light. Zealously, Elias keeps both eyes open lest anyone put anything on the altar but the body of Christ and the gospel book. "The altar," he always says, "is Christ!" Then, correcting himself, "It's the sign of Christ." One day, when the bishop was celebrating there and placed his skullcap on the altar at the beginning of the preface, Elias nimbly snatched it and shoved it into his pocket. "Well done!" Theophilus chuckled to himself. "When I'm invited to dinner, do I put my hat on the dining room table?" Elias also wants the altar to be surrounded with the deepest respect. He sometimes tells about the Copts in Egypt, who remove their shoes before entering the sanctuary and, when they celebrate, never turn their back to the altar but walk backward instead. Of

---

[6]*Order of the Mass*, 101.

course, he has no desire to "Coptify" the Roman Mass, but he does ask the people to draw inspiration from the spirit of these ancient liturgies.

While the bread and wine are being presented, Theophilus recollects himself in the Lord. "The Eucharist is nothing," he muses, "love is all. Or, rather, the Eucharist is all if it expresses love." Their parish has become a community of love and sharing, and each celebration kindles an immense fire of charity. "A Mass," he continues, "is a success, not because the singing was beautiful—what do notes matter compared to charity?—but because we've grown in brotherly love."

Father Elias has urged his parish not to withdraw into a kind of spiritual self-seeking, but to open its heart to human suffering throughout the world. As a result, they have adopted a small Christian village in Upper Egypt, which is still living as in the days of Abraham, a mission being founded in French Guiana, as well as several Indian families and five lepers, in whom they take a personal interest. (Whenever missionary priests or nuns pass through, he invites them to share the joys and sorrows of their apostolate with the community.) For this parish, the entire world has become an altar of glory—and sometimes a Calvary, too—for mankind's Eucharist.

Theophilus used to wonder whether, instead of bread and wine for the Eucharist, one could use other elements: the staple foods of the country in question. For instance, in the Guianan mission which the parish has taken under its wing, the Indians bake millet-flour biscuits that look deceptively like bread. Could these be used at Mass? When questioned, Father Elias had remained prudently evasive: "To celebrate the sacrament is to do again what Christ wanted us to do again. Now, he took bread and wine—not rice or maize, not beer or tea. Therefore, we take bread and wine." Realizing, on second thought, that this argument seemed rather like begging the question, he had continued, thinking aloud, "The whole problem is precisely to know what Jesus wanted when he said, 'Take and eat.' Did he mean 'Take *bread* and eat' or simply 'Take and eat as you celebrate a *meal*'? In the first case, it's the bread and the wine that were instituted as 'signs' of the sacrament, and we must take bread and wine again until the parousia. In the second, it's the meal that becomes the 'sign' of the sacrament, and the Guianan mission can take its biscuits of millet, manioc or rice. While we're at it, another inevitable question is this: Which solution comes closer to the Gospel? Did the Lord of freedom, who burst the bonds of ancient formalism, wish to impose such rubrical fetters for the sacrament of his love? Did the defender of the poor specify, for the feast of the lowly, a food and beverage of the rich, brought to Guiana not in the name of the Gospel, but simply thanks to Air France? And, lastly, which solution is more profoundly in line with the incarnation? Jesus took bread because he was living in Israel and had become incarnate in the life of his people. (I shudder to think that if he'd been born in China, my Gallic ancestors and I would have had to use tea, though we're Burgundians—and of the best vintage!) But seriously, to continue the movement of the incarnation, to incarnate the Church in a country, is to take that country's equivalent of bread and wine, that country's particular 'fruit of the earth and work of human hands.' If only the Church would state her preference for the bread of the poor. . . . But the question isn't ripe yet. Still, under the sun of the Spirit and the warmth of freedom, things can ripen fast. . . ." At that moment, Theophilus could sense what Elias wanted: the most incarnate liturgy possible, the kind closest to the people—and, therefore, closest to God's heart as well.

The Eucharistic acclamations

How else can we describe the Eucharistic Prayer except to say it is the most festive moment of the Mass, the moment when the people participate most intensely? In the past, from the *Sanctus* to the *Pater*, it seemed as though a pall of sadness descended on the monologuing priest and the silent congregation. But since the Eucharistic acclamations were inserted into the prayer, not to interrupt but to support the president's words, the effect is always one of joyful celebration. Theophilus is especially fond of the acclamation for this Sunday: "Give thanks to the Lord, for he is good; his love is everlasting!"—the very refrain Jesus sang at the last supper.

What Jesus said was this: "Do this in memory of me." He did not say, "Do something boring in memory of me." Neither did he say, "The more you Christian people, my friends, appear sad, the more seriously the world will accept my message!" Did not Jesus come to us in order that our joy—his joy in us (John 15:11)—be complete? In his face there was the smile of heaven. That was what attracted the children of the gospel. And at the last supper he celebrated a festive meal and sang hymns with his apostles. "My God," Theophilus reflects, "it is the joy of Christians which will convert the world to you. It is laughing and dancing in our celebrations that will reveal your face, O Jesus!" Surely, this does not mean ignoring the tear-furrowed faces we see among us—sometimes through our own tears: the earth is full of tombs! But it means believing that God's promise holds true: "I am now going to open your graves; I mean to raise you from your graves, my people!" (Ezekiel 37:12). Above all, it means pledging oneself at each Mass, in the name of God's love for the world, to start then and there opening those tombs—of anxiety, of solitude, of despair—in which we are all imprisoned.

At each elevation, Theophilus humbly venerates the body of the Lord. He knows that, according to Western theology, the real presence begins when the words of consecration end. And he distrusts an acquaintance who once told him, "The consecration is all or nothing. The priest says 'This,' and there's nothing; he says 'is'—nothing; 'my'—still nothing; then he says 'body,' and suddenly it's all there!" To Theophilus, that seems like reducing the words of consecration to some sort of magician's formula. "And what about Christ's presence in the Word (p. 119) and in the assembly (p. 115)?" he asks rhetorically. "Isn't that a real presence, too? Father tells me the Eastern tradition stresses the consecrating power of the epiclesis: for them, it's the invocation of the Spirit that makes Christ sacramentally present. I don't much care for these discussions where timetables and stopwatches take the place of theology. As far as I'm concerned, the Eucharistic Prayer is one and indivisible. Naturally, it takes a while to say: after all, we're not God, and so we have to put one word after another and say over a span of time what he can say in a single word in an instant."

Celebrating together

At a concelebrated Mass not long ago, Theophilus was very surprised to hear the seven concelebrants recite the words of consecration together. He simply could not understand this rubrical oddity. As he was rightly taught, the celebration should reflect the very structure of the ecclesial community. Now, the Church is a very harmonious and admirably structured body—"as lovely as a bride," says Scripture. Being a harmonious body, she should have only one head—that is, only one president acting in the name of Jesus Christ. And he who presides is not above the others: he is merely performing a ministry; for it is the entire community (a "priestly" people, as we read in 1 Peter 2:9) which "concelebrates," each according to his rank—the priests as priests, and the faithful as faithful. But there, in that celebration with seven presidents, one received the impression, not so much of a single celebration, as of priests saying their individual Masses simultaneously in an atmosphere of clerical triumphalism. May he be forgiven such impertinence, but Theophilus immediately thought of the seven-headed beast in the Book of Revelation (12:3).

A liturgy still being perfected

Father Elias often says, "I've got to admit the present liturgy isn't perfect. But it's progressing. We've come a long way in ten years! Just remember those Masses before the Council, when—in important centers, like places of pilgrimage—each priest used to celebrate at a separate altar the sacrifice that was supposed to affirm the Church's unity! So, if now and then we can look ahead at the road yet to be covered and wish some things would move faster, we also have to admire the renewal which the Spirit of Jesus hasn't stopped generating. Who would have thought that a Church so ossified in her rubrics, so drowsy in her habits, could be so thoroughly rejuvenated? Why, it's a real springtime!"

Traditionalists and innovators

In a parish Theophilus knows but prefers not to mention, the whole community recites the Eucharistic Prayer together. What an idea! It makes about as much sense as having the whole assembly read the gospel together under the pretext of greater participation! "Such bungling innovations," Theophilus believes, "sell the liturgy short. Those who take such steps are as much to blame as those who, in their loyalty to the past, refuse to move ahead. The traditionalists embalm the corpses from the past; the bungling innovators deliver them to the crematory. Both work with the dead."

But Theophilus notes, "In our parish we are going along in God's today—not lagging, not hurrying. We walk hand in hand with Christ, helping the whole ecclesial community to move ahead.

"Even if we don't always agree with the authorities, even if they tend to side with the footdragging lovers of the past instead of those who carry on the research that made renewal possible, our free obedience is the price we pay for unity. But, most of all, we mustn't confuse the institution with the Church: for the institution is bound to suffer the stiffness of old age in its members, but the Church—which Scripture never portrays as an old lady, but as a young girl, the pure virgin betrothed to Christ—retains her dazzling youth, spontaneously creative, joyfully searching and exuberantly alive. And that Church is each one of us!"[7]

Waiting for the Lord

Theophilus is very fond of the memorial acclamation, that song of hope which proclaims, "We're waiting for you to re-

---

[7]To complete Theophilus' thinking, one might say that the juridical problem posed is that of a liberal statute concerning research and development in the Church. This would relieve much unnecessary tension.

turn, O Lord," and proves that the Christian community has dwelling in it the Spirit, who whispers in its heart, "Come, Lord Jesus!" (Revelation 22:20). In point of fact, Theophilus' church has something in common with all the ancient cathedrals in France: it is oriented—that is to say, its chancel faces the Orient, the east. "Too bad," sighs Theophilus, "that our civilization, taken up as it is with electricity, isn't more alive to this symbolism! Personally, I'm kind of a heliotropic soul—in love with the sun! And when I go to church on a Sunday morning and see the sanctuary flooded with sunlight, I know the Christian community is a community of hope, waiting for the never-ending day when the risen Christ will appear, like the never-setting sun" (p. 61).

With the saints, our friends

Also marvelous is the prayer after the consecration which recalls the Virgin Mary, the apostles, the martyrs and all the saints, as well as parents and friends already dwelling in the light of God, where they celebrate the eternal Eucharist. "Here we are"—and Theophilus rejoices at the thought—"sitting at the same table with them, communicating with the same Lord— they in the radiance of face-to-face vision, and we in the half-light of faith." As he ponders, his mind ranges further: "This bread and wine conjure up the whole history of Israel, too—all those countless thousands who repeated the gestures of love between man and woman so that eventually the body of Jesus might be born. And this cup mysteriously contains the blood of Ruth, the 'daughter' of an alien god; the blood of Tamar, who played the prostitute in order to have children; and the blood of Rahab, who really was one; not counting the blood of that other ancestor of Jesus'—Bathsheba, the adulteress. Yes, Jesus had in his veins the blood of a courtesan and of an adulteress! But he also had the blood of that flower of Israel, that marvel of grace, whose splendor redeemed all ugliness—the Virgin Mary. All those names shine like diamonds when we read the genealogy of the Messiah in Matthew's Gospel. To think that herein, in the

Eucharist, we commune with all that history of Israel's! What's more, we add our own personal history—and it's transfigured into thanksgiving, into Eucharist. Saint Augustine writes somewhere[8] that, at communion, when the priest says, 'The body of Christ,' and we answer, 'Amen,' we're actually speaking our own name, since we truly become the Lord's body."

COMMUNION, A SHARING OF LOVE

Theophilus and Philothea enjoy taking communion side by side. Father Elias gives them a single piece of consecrated bread and they share it. If they are man and wife, is it not in order that they should give each other Jesus Christ? When they married, people around them remarked, "They are a real pair." In fact, the name Theo-philus means the same thing as Philo-thea: God-lover, lover-of-God.

Witness of St. Cyril today

For quite a while now they have been receiving the body of the Lord in their hands. They are astonished to hear that, in some countries, this way of communion is still a matter of debate. They remember having read somewhere a beautiful text of St. Cyril of Jerusalem (died c. 387): "When you come up to receive the Lord, make of your left hand a throne for your right, the hand which is to receive the King. Receive the body of Christ in the palm of your hand and answer 'Amen' . . . Then, after having received the body of Christ, go over to the chalice of his blood. Do not reach out, but bow in a gesture of adoration and veneration and answer 'Amen' . . . Then, while waiting for the prayer, give thanks to God, who has deemed you worthy of so great a mystery."[9] After reading those words, who can consider communion in the hand something new?

[8]*Sermon 272.*
[9]*Mystagogical Catecheses*, V, 21-22.

Drinking from the cup

Theophilus also enjoys receiving communion from the cup of the Lord. He has always wondered why theologians have bent all their cunning to the task of proving that, in communion, taking bread is enough. True, Christ is present under the single species with body, blood, soul and divinity. Surely Christ was as aware of this as the theologians; yet he said, "Take this and *eat it*; take this and *drink it.*" Theophilus does not like it when theology replaces the gospel or theologians seem more learned than Jesus. He prefers them to put themselves at the Lord's service to show that it is preferable to receive communion the way Christ wanted it to be received.

Yet he understands why Mr. Farber does not take the cup. Mr. Farber lives in fear of germs and is constantly disinfecting his mouth, his nose, his throat and everything else. Theophilus isn't afraid of catching anything. He read in a magazine that there is no more danger of catching something from the chalice than there is of catching something riding in the bus, where the rate of germ exchange is extremely high. He takes the bus to work every morning, and he is in pretty good health!

Theophilus knows that, in certain Eastern rites, the faithful do not receive directly from the chalice. The priest practices intinction—dipping the consecrated bread into the wine and then giving it to the faithful. Theophilus has profound respect for the Eastern rites, and especially for intinction, but he does not care for it for himself. He remembers that Christ said, "Take this bread and eat it; take this wine and drink it," not "Take this bread and dunk it."

Like a cloak of splendor

Today, after the communion processional, the choir is singing like a choir of angels. Its ministerial function is to "edify," that is, to "build." And, in fact, the choir has built an "environment" (as we say when we want to appear well instructed) of joy, peace, beauty. They dress the liturgy in a cloak of splendor.

Father Elias says that now, more than ever, the parish needs a good choir. He is fortunate to have an excellent choirmaster, Mr. Melody, who enjoys working with him, pulling the parochial chariot in the same direction. Sometimes he smiles and groans simultaneously: "Before Vatican II there was never as much singing and playing of music as we have now in the Church. We sing as a choir alone and along with the people, in parts and in unison. We sing constantly!" But he delights in the consideration that Father Elias and the community give the choir. Some say singing tires tnem; but for a Christian, can there be a more delicious fatigue than singing for the Lord? Long ago the choir left the loft and is now located between the congregation and the sanctuary.

"Populo dimisso . . ."

Theophilus is not surprised that, after communion, the priest does not purify the cups or patens or trays. He knows that "it is permitted to wash the vessels after the *populo dimisso*"[10]—that is, after the people have gone. It is easy to see that the washing of the vessels is not a great liturgical action! And Theophilus cannot understand talk of "purification." As if the body of the Risen Christ could soil anything! He knows that the Lord is sacramentally present as long as the *sign* of bread persists, but not in crumbs the size of tiny specks of white dust. In any case, he does not care to watch the celebrant "doing the dishes" as he faces the assembly and then drinking the dishwater.

It is the old story of overdoing ritual acts by giving them too much importance. And it shows too little respect for the altar, which is a sign of Christ, not a scullery table. Anyway, as Theophilus knows, Sister Adelpha takes care of everything in the sacristy; everything will be tidied up after Mass in conformity with the rubrics.

---

[10] *Order of the Mass*, 120.

The Mass in our life

Usually, after Mass, Theophilus and Philothea join the people who gather in the room adjoining the church to say "hello" to those they did not have a chance to greet at Mass. They also have a cup of coffee.

But today Father Elias asks Theophilus to take communion to Mrs. Marie Martin, a little old lady in the neighborhood who lives alone. In addition to her ordinary work, she used to do works of mercy, discreetly, so that even her left hand did not know what her right hand was doing. No one knew of the many troubles she had smoothed out. Now she is semiparalyzed and waiting for the Lord, "to greet him when he comes again," as the Mass says. Behind her window drapes she is on the lookout for Theophilus and his wife. At last, they arrive!

For them, this is a moving experience. Theophilus says to Marie, "I am bringing you the Lord—God's bread sent by the whole community. They are thinking of you. The Duponts will be visiting tomorrow. Once it was you who went to meet the Lord; today he comes to you!" Then he gives her communion, according to the *Ritual* that Father Elias gave him. He reads the Gospel, and the three of them share a bit of a homily.

Then Theophilus and Philothea take Marie home with them to lunch. As Philothea says, "You have shared the bread of heaven with us; now you must share with us at home the bread of earth, and the wine and the joy of this Lord's day!"

Marie's own Mass

In the afternoon, the trio goes to the park. As dear old Marie sees the children playing in the grass with Snoopy, as she catches the aroma of moss among the trees and watches the oak leaves shiver with pleasure, she murmurs, "O my soul, bless the Lord!"

Her whole life has been her own personal Mass, a life going its peaceful way like a spring evening. Her altar has been the busses and the streets of the town, her kitchen, her sink, her ironing board, her workroom and her typewriter, with a few lilies of the valley to brighten up the place. In a lyric mood, she pursues her thoughts: "It will soon be the Eternal Day, the Day of the Lord that has no evening. Then I will be at ease; I will see you forever, Lord. I will see and love you forever. I will love and praise you forever."[11] And she adds, "But right now, thank you, Lord, for allowing me to see the joy of springtime in nature. Thank you, Lord, for allowing me to live in the springtime of your Church."

*   *

*

---

[11]Without knowing it, Marie is paraphrasing Saint Augustine, *The City of God*, XXII, 30, 5.

FOREST BOOKS

PORTRAIT OF THE ARTIST
AS AN ABOMINABLE SNOWMAN

GABRIEL ROSENSTOCK was born in 1949. He now lives in
Dublin with his wife and four children, and works with An Gúm,
an all Irish language publishing house. He is also a noted broad-
caster and writer for children. Currently he is Chairman of Poetry
Ireland and has recently been given an Arts Council Bursary and
the Irish-American Cultural Foundation award. His first volume
was published in 1973 and since then he has written six other
books of poetry.

MICHAEL HARTNETT is well known as a poet both in English
and in Irish. He has translated poetry from the Irish, Spanish and
Hungarian.

JASON SOMMER is an American poet, translator and teacher.

Gabriel Rosenstock

PORTRAIT OF THE
ARTIST AS AN
ABOMINABLE SNOWMAN

Selected poems by Gabriel Rosenstock
Translated from the Irish by Michael Hartnett
and New Poems
Translated by Jason Sommer

FOREST BOOKS
LONDON * 1989 * BOSTON

20 Forest View, Chingford, London E4 7 AY, U.K.
PO Box 438, Wayland, MA 01778, U.S.A.

First Published 1989

Typeset in the Republic of Ireland by Cristina Ní
Chualáin
Printed in Great Britain by BPCC Wheatons Ltd, Exeter

Translations © Michael Hartnett (Selected poems)
Jason Sommer (New Poems)
Cover design © Ann Evans
Original Work © Gabriel Rosenstock

British Library Cataloguing in Publication Data
Rosenstock, Gabriel
Portrait of the artist as an abominable snowman:
selected poems from the Irish
I. Title.   II. Hartnett, Michael, 1941
III. Sommer, Jason
891. 6'214

ISBN 0 948259 56 6

Library of Congress Catalogue Card No
88–083646

Photo by Bill Doyle

The word is a psyche. The living word does not signify an object, but freely chooses, as though for a dwelling place, this or that objective significance, materiality, some beloved body. And around the thing the word hovers freely, like a soul around a body that has been abandoned but not forgotten . . .

Osip Mandelstam in *The Word and Culture* (1921)

Contents

NEW POEMS

Béal Séad	10
Belshade	11
An Móta i gCill Fhíonáin	12
The Moat in Kilfinane	13
Eisreachtaí	14
Outlaw	15
Cloigeann	16
The Head	17
Srannadh agus Rumi	18
Snoring and Rumi	19
An Bhean a Thit i nGrá le Dracula	20
The Woman Who Fell in Love with Dracula	21
An Mhaenad	22
The Maenad	23
Mo Ghrá Bán	24
My Fair Love	25
Rahu	26
Rahu	27
Cleacht an Claon	32
Practice Deceit	33
Ómós	34
Homage	35
Portráid den Ealaíontóir mar Yeti	36
Portrait of the Artist as an Abominable Snowman	37

SELECTED POEMS

In Íoclann M'Athar Cúig Bliana is Fiche Ó Shin	40
My Father's Dispensary: 25 Years Ago	41
Nóiméid Uaireanta	42
Minutes/Hours	43
Ravi Shankar	46
Ravi Shankar	47
Rabharta	48
Torrent	49

Ag Obair ar Théacsleabhar sa Ghúm	50
Textbook: An Gúm	51
Brahms	52
Brahms	53
Billie Holiday	54
Billie Holiday	55
Dom Sheanchara, Tom Goggin	56
For My Old Friend, Tom Goggin	57
Dom Chomhfhilí	58
To My Fellow Poets	59
Koan	60
Koan	61
Do Meg	62
For Meg	63
Ag Filleadh ar an nGúm	64
Returning to the Gúm	65
Cailín Scoile i Séipéal	66
School-Girl in Chapel	67
Plandaí Bialainne	68
Plants in a Restaurant	69
Giorriacha	70
Hares	71
Uamhan	72
Fear	73
Rún na gCat	74
Secrets	75
Cléithín	76
Splint	77
Bó Lascaux	78
Lascaux Cow	79
Scáthanna	80
Shadows	81
Séasúr	82
Season	83
Lay of an Outcast Indian	84
Dry Martini Weekend	89
I Open my Poem	91
Clock	93
Sometimes I'm a Liar	94
Soft and Hard	97
Onkel Otto	98
Television	99

Hymn   100
Pursuit   101
Shelley   104
'And If Thine Eye Causeth Thee To Stumble,
     Pluck It Out . . .'   105
Sea-Hymn   106
Phantom Needles   107
Woman in Wheelchair   108

Selected poems are drawn from the following volumes: *Susanne Sa Seomra Folctha, Tuirlingt, OM, Méaram, Nihil Obstat, Rún na gCaisleán,* and *Migmars.*

New Poems

BELSHADE (BÉAL SÉAD)

Áitreabhaigh an tí seo romhainn
Bhogadar go Sasana iad beirt sna hochtóidí.
Scríobhadar chugainn díreach le rá
Go raibh súil acu go mbeimisne chomh sona ann
Is a bhí siadsan
Agus *Belshade*, ainm an tí,
Ar eagla nach ndúradar linn é,
Loch beag i dTír Chonaill atá ann.
Tá fonn orm an t-ainm a fhágáil mar atá
B'fhéidir an loch féin a aimsiú lá éigin
Agus smaoineamh ar an tseanlánúin
Iad óg lúfar
Ag suirí cois locha
Nó ag smearadh ime ar cheapaire
Ag mionallagar le chéile
Faoin aimsir, na séaduiscí, na scamaill.
Na bláthanna a chuireadar
Tá cuid díobh nár dhreoigh
Ainneoin an tseaca.
Tá lorg strainséirí faram lá agus oíche
Agus uaireanta is léire iad ná cairde cnis.

BELSHADE

The previous owners of this house
Went off to England, both of them in their eighties.
They wrote to us just to say
They hoped we would be happy here
As they had been
And *Belshade*, the name of the house,
In case they hadn't told us
Is a small lake in Donegal.
I'm half inclined to leave the name as it is
Maybe discover the lake someday
And think of the old couple
Young and lithe
Courting by the lake
Or spreading butter on a sandwich
Chatting idly to one another
About the weather, the jewelled waters, the clouds.
Some of the flowers that they planted
Have not withered
Despite the frost.
The trace of strangers is around me day and night
And is clearer sometimes than close friends.

AN MÓTA I gCILL FHÍONÁIN

Is dóigh liom gur tuigeadh dom
I bhfad siar go mairfeadh sé inár ndiaidh
Go raibh sé níos ársa, níos buaine
Ná caismirt bhinn na gcamán.
Bhí nithe thart orainn is sinn ag éirí aníos
A bheannaigh sinn le milseacht agus uamhan:
Tobar beannaithe ... an dtrialltar a thuilleadh air?
Teampall Gallda; (chloistí slabhraí sa reilig
I gcorplár na hoíche!)
Agus an móta –
Macalla rúndiamhair balbh ó ghlóir-réim
Dhearmadta na staire.
Bhí radharc agat óna bharr
Ar thailte méithe Luimnigh
Scamall scinnideach thar chnoc crannach
Seanchú dearóil á ghrianadh féin os comhair an
   fhochla
Agus istoíche na réaltaí
Ag stánadh anuas ar an móta
Faoi mar ba dhílleachta leo é.

Ba é ár dTeamhair féin é, déanta na fírinne,
Croílár na cruinne.

12

THE MOAT IN KILFINANE

I think I understoood
Even back then that it would outlive us
That it was more ancient, more permanent
Than the sweet clash of hurleys.
There were things around us when we were
    growing up
That blessed us with sweetness and terror:
A holy well ... do they still visit it?
A Protestant church; (chains were heard in the
    graveyard
In the dead of night!)
And the moat –
Mute, mysterious echo
Of the forgotten historical pageant.
You had a view from the top
Of the fertile plains of Limerick
A flighty cloud over a wooded hill
A miserable old greyhound sunning himself in
    front of the grotto
And at night the stars
Looking down on the moat
As though on their orphan.

It was our own Tara, if the truth be told,
The deep heart of the universe.

EISREACHTAÍ
(Don ealaíontóir, Sir Sidney Nolan)

Bealach na Bó Finne istoíche
De chaoirigh ag mungailt na machairí
Méithe – ní dúchasach a méileach:
Caithfear triall níos faide siar.

'Sin é an saol,' arsa an t-ógfhear
Ned Kelly ag gáire leis an mbás,
Níor dhúchasach eisean ach an oiread.
Caithfear triall níos faide siar

Níos faide siar fós
Níos mó sa chré ghrianársa
Sna patrúin a bhreactar
Ar chraiceann dóite –
Go croí na mistéire

Fiagaí ag téaltú
Ag teacht aniar aduaidh
Ar an tseilg
Beannaíonn na leoithní é
Cuireann uime ceann díobh mar bhrat
Reonn a chabhail nocht
Is i dtobainne aimsíonn
A dhúchas.

Cad a thit de phlimp phlúchta?
Réalta?
Cangarú?
Eisreachtaí?

OUTLAW
(For the painter, Sir Sidney Nolan)

A milky way of sheep at night
Grazing the fertile plains
Their bleating is not native
One must go further back.

'Such is life,' said the young man
Ned Kelly, laughing at death,
And he wasn't native either.
One must go further back

Still further back
Further still into the sun-ancient earth
Into the patterns mottled
On burnt skin
To the heart of the mystery

A stalking hunter
Surprising
His prey
The breezes bless him
He clothes himself with one of them like a cloak
His naked frame freezes
And in a flash he has discovered
His heritage.

What fell with a muffled thud?
A star?
A kangaroo?
An outlaw?

CLOIGEANN

Cara liom
A thug cuairt
Ar an séipéal
I nDroichead Átha
Ina gcoinnítear
Cloigeann Oilibhéar Pluincéad –
Is é ar tí imeacht
Nár chaoch an tArdeaspag
Súil air!
D'impigh mo chara orm
Gan an scéal a insint d'éinne
Agus ar ór ná ar airgead
Ní sceithfinn a ainm.
Ach dála mhac na baintrí
A chaith rún mór an Rí
A insint do chrann
Gur labhair an chláirseach ar ball:
'Tá cluasa capaill ar Labhraidh Loingseach!'
Fógraímse anseo gur
Chaoch sé súil air
Chaoch sé súil.

THE HEAD

A friend of mine
Who visited
The church
In Drogheda
Where they keep
The head of Oliver Plunkett –
When he was about to go
Didn't the Archbishop
Wink at him!
My friend begged me
Not to tell the story to anyone
And I wouldn't give away his name
For gold or silver.
But as with the widow's son
Who had to tell the king's great secret
To a tree
And the harp said later:
'Labhraidh Loingseach has horse's ears'
I announce here
He winked at him
He winked.

SRANNADH AGUS RUMI

Mo bhean ag srannadh.
(Má léann sí é seo beidh sí ar buile)
Ach nílim buartha.
Dhá uair an chloig caite agam
Ag léamh filíocht Rumi.

An srannadh in airde ar nós colúr
Ar an díon
Ní chuireann sé as dom puinn:

Glór na gaoithe sa simné
Crónán beach, búiríl tonn . . .
Is í an uile fhuaim í.

Raghad in airde go ciúin.

SNORING AND RUMI

My wife snoring
(If she reads this she'll be angry)
But I'm not worried.
I've just spent two hours
Reading Rumi's poems.

The snoring overhead like pigeons
On the roof
Doesn't bother me at all:

The sound of the wind in the chimney
The buzzing of bees, the roaring of waves . . .
She is every sound.

I will go up quietly.

AN BHEAN A THIT I nGRÁ LE DRACULA

Mílítheach mé id dhiaidh, a Chunta,
Ó d'ólais deoch asam
Fuar do theanga ar mo bhráid
Glioscarnach gléigeal do dhéada
Do dhá rosc ionam
Mé ionat
Is leat mé

Siúracha uile na Saoirse
Dá dtuigfidís
Ghearrfaidís a riostaí
Chun tú a ghríosú
Nochtfaidís leathchíoch
A Chunta liom, a ansacht, a mhian,
A Chamhaoir dhearg
A fhuil uasal gan scáth
Fill do sciatháin leathair tharam
Fáisc m'anam asam

THE WOMAN WHO FELL
IN LOVE WITH DRACULA

Count, you have left me pale
Since you drank from me
Your tongue cold on my neck
Your teeth shining bright
Your two eyes in mine
Me in yours
I am yours

All the liberated Sisters
If they understood
They would slash their wrists
To spur you on
Would bare a breast
My count, dearest, desired one
Oh red-dawning
Oh noble fearless blood
Wrap your leathery wings around me
Wring the soul from me

AN MHAENAD

Tá crónán beach dostoptha ina broinn
Nach múchfar ach i dtonn bháite
Go coim.

Seasann an mhaenad sa sáile
Rud doráite
Ina súile ar déanamh na halmóinne.

Gortóidh sobal goirt a pit ata
Ar ball agus gáirfidh sí,
Cúbfaidh tonnta óna fraoch.

Titfidh liomúin agus oráistí ina mbáisteach
Léimfidh éisc ildathacha
Agus beifear ar fad ar aon dord.

Níos déanaí
Nochtfaidh réaltaí as an gciúnas
Faoi mar nár tharla faic
Faoi mar a bheadh an chéad chruthú ann.
Fáiscfidh sí smugairle róin lena gabhal.

THE MAENAD

The ceaseless bee-buzzing in her womb
Will not be calmed except
In the waist-high storm waves.

The maenad stands in the sea
Something unsayable
In those eyes the shape of almonds.

Soon salt foam will sting her vulva
And she will laugh
Waves will retreat from her fury.

Lemons and oranges will rain down
Multicoloured fish will leap
And all will be in one humming unison.

Later
Stars will emerge from the stillness
As though nothing had happened
As though it were the first creation.
She'll press a jellyfish to her crotch.

MO GHRÁ BÁN

Do thaibhse iarshuirí meallann fós mé
Do chruth fágtha ar an mbráillín

Siúd na ceathrúna
Go soiléir cnámh an chromáin
Cíocha, colpaí
Chomh mealltach céanna
D'fhágais marbhmhasc beo
Do cholainne
Ar an leaba

Mua

MY FAIR LOVE

Your ghost after love tempts me
Your shape left in the sheets

There are the thighs
Clearly the hip bone
Breasts, calves
As tempting as ever

You left the living death mask
Of your body
On the bed

Phantom

RAHU

I
Rahu
Deamhan
A shlogann
Gealach
Is grian
Slog
Éiclips
Mo mheabhrach
Urlaic mé
Ansin
Ar thrá
Faoi réaltaí
Rahu
D'éireoinn
Shiúlfainn
Mholfainn
Déithe
Is deamhain

II
Rahu
Oighear
Do phóg
Sioc
Do theanga
Cloch
Do rosc
Gaoth fhuar
D'anáil
Broigheall
Ar charraig
Níl éalú
Uait

RAHU .

I
Rahu
Demon
That swallows
Moon
And sun
Swallow
The eclipse
Of my mind
Spew me
Then
On a beach
Under stars
Rahu
I would arise
I would walk
I would praise
Gods
And demons

II
Rahu
Ice
Your kiss
Frost
Your tongue
A stone
Your eye
A cold wind
Your breath
A cormorant
On a rock
No escaping
You

27

Fiú
I nduibheagán
Snámh
Chugam
Alp

III
Rahu
Scairtim
Ort
Ní heol
Dom
Aon
Deamhan
Eile
Tá
Naoimh
Uile
Neimhe
Ag canadh
Iomann
Is Dia
Bodhar
Ag éisteacht
Leo
Ach
Taoise
Id dhúiseacht
Ag faire
Ar ghealach
Is grian
Meall cruinn
Sa spéir
Mé
Oscail
Do chraos

28

Even
In a black abyss
Swim
To me
Devour

III
Rahu
I call
On you
I know
No other
Demon
All
Heaven's
Saints
Are singing
Hymns
And
God
Deaf
From listening
To them
But
You are
Awake
Watching
The moon
And sun
I am
A round
Shape
In the
Sky
Open
Your throat

29

IV
Oscail
Oscail
Chodlóinn
Go cluthair
Id dhuibhe
Athchruthaigh
Id bholg mé
Díleáigh
Mo smaointe
Folmhú
Do phutóige
Ba cheol dom
Rahu
Ba mheadaracht
Gluaiseacht
Na matán
Ainneonach

V
Rahu
Níl fhios
Agam
An gcloisir
Nó ar labhair
Aon daonnaí
Riamh leat
Cheana
Glac
Lem ghuí
Slog
Is
Caith
Amach
Mé
Rahu
Deamhan

IV

Open
Open
Cosily
I would sleep
In your darkness
Re-make me
In your belly
Digest
My thoughts
The voiding
Of your bowels
Would be music to me
Metre
The movement
Of involuntary
Muscles

V

Rahu
I know not
If you can hear
Or whether any human
Ever spoke to you
Before
Accept
My prayer
Devour
And
Throw
Me
Up
Rahu
Demon

CLEACHT AN CLAON

"Is mé an Fhírinne,"
arsa Sufi Hallaj
agus chuireadar
chun báis é.

Tá sé priaclach go leor
an fhírinne a insint
ach más tú an Fhírinne
b'fhearr duit do chlab
a choimeád dúnta.

Fiú ansin
sceithfeadh an fhírinne
ó do shúile

Bheadh sí ina
luan os do chionn
chanfadh fuiseoga
thuirlingeoidís ort
neadóidís id fhéasóg
bheifeá ar nós mo dhuine i luimneach úd Lear.
Cleacht an claon
is é is sábháilte.

PRACTICE DECEIT

"I am the Truth,"
said Sufi Hallaj
And they put him
to death.

It is dangerous enough
to tell the truth
but if you are the Truth
you had better keep
your trap shut.

Even then
truth would escape
from your eyes

And form a halo
over you
larks would sing
they would alight on you
they would nest in your beard
you'd be like the man in Lear's limerick.
Practice deceit
it's safer.

ÓMÓS

Níl aon chuid den eilifint
Nach n-itheann na pigmithe –
Srí Ganesha Namah!
Piocann siad amach an smior
Is alpann amh é
Srí Ganeshaya Namah!
Níl aon chuid den dufair
Nach gcritheann ag an treascairt
Srí Ganeshaya Namah!
Canann bás na heilifinte an bheatha:
Seo, déanaigí a dhuilleoga gairdeas
Is a ghrian ag saighdeadh tríothu
OM Srí Ganeshya Namah!

Is geall le dia an eilifint
Is geall le sliabh
Is geall le toirneach
Iompraíonn a chuid starrfhiacla an domhan
Is a bhfuil ann
Srí Ganeshaya Namah!
Seo ... ithimis agus ólaimis aisti ...
Seo é smúsach Dé
OM Srí Ganeshaya Namah!

HOMAGE

There is no part of the Elephant
Which the Pygmies do not eat –
Sri Ganesha Namah!
They pick out the marrow
And swallow it raw
Sri Ganeshaya Namah!
There is no part of the jungle
Which does not tremble at this downfall
Sri Ganeshaya Namah!
The elephant's death sings life:
Come leaves rejoice
And sun which arrows through
OM Sri Ganeshaya Namah!

The Elephant is like a god
Like a mountain
Like thunder
His tusks carry the world
And all that is in it
Sri Ganeshaya Namah!
Come ... let us eat and drink of it ...
This, the pith of God
OM Sri Ganeshaya Namah!

PORTRÁID DEN EALAÍONTÓIR MAR YETI

Tuirsíonn na Himáilithe mé ba mhaith liom
Teachín i gConamara
(Is clos dom nach dtiteann puinn sneachta ann)
An sean-nós a fhoghlaim
Bréidín a chaitheamh, móin a bhaint, piontaí a ól,
  dul ar an dól.
Deir Sir Edmund Hillary nach ann dom
Ach tá rún agam labhairt ar Raidió na Gaeltachta
Agus é a bhréagnú. (Bastart de Bhrit).

Tuirsíonn na Himáilithe mé gan de chomhluadar
  agam
Ach naoimh i bpluaiseanna (chuirfidís soir tú)
Nach labhraíonn le héinne
Ach Dia amháin OM OM ó dhubh go dubh.
Tuirsíonn loinnir neamhshaolta a súl mé
Agus loinnir ghorm an oighir.
Ba mhaith liom Gaeilge a fhoghlaim go paiteanta
A bheith ar an gcéad Yeti riamh
(Agus an Yeti deireanach)
Ar fhoireann an Acadaimh Ríoga.

Dá mbainfinn féin amach trí mhíorúilt éigin
Inis aoibhinn Ealga
An nglacfaí liom
Nó an ndéanfadh monarcha éigin
De chuid Údarás na Gaeltachta
Cairpéad bán dem chuid fionnaidh?
Tuirsíonn na Himáilithe mé róghar do Neamh
Rófhada uaithi mo léir
Ní duine ná ainmhí mé is nárbh aoibhinn bheith
  slogtha ag an spéir.

PORTRAIT OF THE ARTIST AS AN
ABOMINABLE SNOWMAN

I'm tired of the Himalayas I'd like
A cottage in Connemara
(I hear that no snow falls there)
Learn sean-nós singing, wear home-spun, dig turf,
  drink pints, go on the dole.
Sir Edmund Hillary says I don't exist
But I intend to go on Raidió na Gaeltachta
And prove him wrong. (British bastard).

I'm tired of the Himalayas – no company
Except for holy men in caves (they'd drive you
    crazy)
Who speak to no one
Only God OM OM from morning till night.
I'm tired of the cosmic shimmer of their eyes
And the blue shine of ice.
I would like to learn perfect Irish
And be the first Yeti ever
(And the last Yeti)
On the staff of the Royal Irish Academy.

If I should find my way through some miracle
To that noble island
Would I be accepted
Or would some Gaeltacht Authority factory
Make a white carpet of my fur?
I'm tired of the Himalayas – too near heaven
Too far away, alas.
I'm neither animal nor human and how I wish
That the sky would swallow me.

Selected Poems

IN ÍOCLANN M'ATHAR
CÚIG BLIANA IS FICHE Ó SHIN

Cúltortann gluaisrothar lasmuigh
Láithreach táim ar ais i gCill Fhionáin.
Raidhfil ina ghlac
Ag m'athair romham san íoclann –
    'An raibh t'athairse in Arm na Gearmáine?'
    'Bhí ach dochtúir a bhí ann . . . síochánaí . . .'
    'Chuala gur mharaigh sé suas le leathchéad Rúiseach!'
    'Bréag –'
Méar ar an truicear, dúnann súil amháin.
Scréach ansin óm Mham; ach tá a guth i gcéin
Is níl aon tarrtháil
Dom féin ná don fhrancach ina phleist ar an urlár.
Sásamh agus alltacht ag satailt ar a chéile,
Mo shúile ar bior. Ní thuigim fós cén fáth
Ar fáiltíodh roimh an gcuairteoir seo le piléar.
Sábháil é! Tá cógais a théarnaimh anseo in aice láimhe.
Las an lampa fodhearg, oscail na buidéil!
Ródhéanach. Siúd romhat an t-éag.
  B'in an chéad mharú
  An chéad cheacht báis; m'athair a mhúin.

MY FATHER'S DISPENSARY : 25 YEARS AGO

Outside a motor-cycle backfires
and suddenly I am in Kilfinane.
In the dispensary my father's before me
armed with a rifle.
  'Was your father in the German Army?'
  'He was, but he was a doctor, a pacifist ...'
  ' 'Tis said he killed up to fifty Russians!'
  'Lies, lies!'
Finger on trigger, he closes one eye.
My mother screams but her voice is distant
and is no help
for me nor for the rat splattered on the floor.
Satisfaction and savagery trample each other
in my eyes agog. I do not understand still
why a bullet greeted this visitor.
Save him! Medicine to cure him is here at hand.
Light the infra-red lamp, open the bottles!
Too late. This is death before you.
  That was the first killing,
  the first lesson in death.
  My father taught me it.

NÓIMÉID UAIREANTA

Foiche lá fearthainne
A glóirín
Múchta

    Préachán
    Trí chuirtín lása
    Nó a scáth

Cac úr éan
Maisíonn
Casán bréan

    As tobar dúigh spéire
    Líonann crainn
    A ngoib

I ngloiní dú' an daill
Dul faoi
Na gréine

    Smólach
    Ar an bhfaiche
    Cigire nóiníní

Bláthanna i vása
Siúlann cat
Trí gharraí lom

MINUTES/HOURS

Wasp on a wet day
Her small voice
Smothered

    Rook
    Through a lace curtain –
    Or its shadow

Fresh birdshit
Adorns
A putrid footpath

    From the sky's ink-well
    Trees fill
    Their nibs

In the blind man's glasses
The setting of
The sun

    Thrush
    On the lawn –
    Daisy-inspector

Flowers in a vase
A cat walks through
A bare garden

Conamara
Chaitheas cat marbh thar chlaí . . .
Réaltaí

Cith tobann fómhair
Féileacán ag dul ar fothain
Faoi dhuilleog

Préacháin
Roimh am bricfeasta
Brách-brách go brách

Connemara
I threw a dead cat over a hedge . . .
Stars

Sudden autumn shower.
Butterfly shelters
Under a leaf

Rooks
Before breakfast
Caw-caw constantly

RAVI SHANKAR

Glaonn
Tú
Anuas
Ó
Na spéartha
Chugainn
Ealaí
Is druideanna
Tá
An domhan
Ina
Aigéan
Cluichearnachta
Níl
Mórthír
Le fáil ...
Stopann
Anáil.

RAVI SHANKAR

You
Call down
From the
Skies
Swans
And starlings
To us
The world's
A fluttering
Ocean
No
Land
Can
Be seen
Breathing stops.

RABHARTA

Tar éis dúinn scor
Dár suirí
Cromadh ar chatachas
Sa chlós:
Dúraís 'Fán fada orthu,
Dúiseofar an leanbh.'
Comharsa linn
A chuir scoiteach
Iontu is idir
An dá linn
Bádh ár seomra
I rabharta ciúin
Gealaí.

TORRENT

Unclasping
after love-making
caterwauling
began in the yard.
You said: 'Blast them anyway,
they'll wake the baby.'
A neighbour
scattered them
and in the meantime
our room was drowned
in a torrent
of moonlight.

AG OBAIR AR THÉACSLEABHAR SA GHÚM

Ba mhaith leat an obair seo a dhéanamh níos
  suimiúla
Ar chuma éigin
Duit féin
Agus do dhaoine eile
Ach caitheadh suim an doras amach
Is daingníodh na boltaí ina coinne.
Ba mhaith leat go léimfeadh rud éigin as gach
  leathanach chugat
Drúchtmhar, drithleach –
Beag an baol
Seasc do shaol.
Ba mhaith leat fonóta a chur leis an iliomad fíricí
Ar eagla go dtógfadh daltaí ródháiríre iad –
Ba mhaith leat a rá leo 'Seachain na carraigeacha
  focal!'
Ach cé tá ag éisteacht?
I gciúnas na maidine titeann dhá chéad páiste le
  haill.

TEXTBOOK: AN GÚM

You would like to make this work
somehow, more interesting
for yourself and for others
but interest goes out the door
and shoots the bolt behind it.
You would like something to leap out of every page,
something dewy, sparkling –
little chance of that:
your life is flat.
You would like to footnote
the myriad facts
for fear students would take them to heart –
You would like to tell them: 'Beware verbal rocks.'
But who is listening?
In the silent morning two hundred children fall from
  clifftops.

BRAHMS

Bhainteá na bróga díot ag teacht isteach
ar eagla go ndúiseofaí an líon tí –
Suanmhar síothach go lá!

Ba rógaire thú i measc cailíní aimsire
ach an bhean ab ansa leat –
'measc na lilí's na mbláth –
Clara, baintreach Schumann,
níor leagais uirthi lámh.

Chuiris olc ar do chairde
in Weimar, Hamburg agus Vín –
thitis amach leat féinig, ní foláir.

Go mbeirse, a stór, gan tuirse, gan bhrón!

Ar leaba do bháis
Chaoin tú uisce do chinn.

BRAHMS

You used to take your shoes off coming in
for fear you'd wake the household –
Guten Abend, gut' Nacht!

You were a rogue with servant-girls
but the woman most dear to you –
Tu' die Auglein zu –
Clara, Schumann's widow,
you never laid a hand on.

You caused your friends ill-feeling
in Weimar, Hamburg and Vienna –
you almost fell out with yourself!

Von Engeln bewacht, schlaf in guter Ruh.

On your death-bed
you lamented
the tears of your head.

BILLIE HOLIDAY

D'fháiscis pian
As sárbhinneas
Binneas
As sárphian
Nuair a éigníodh thú in aois
Do dheich mbliana duit
B'in an chéad tairne
I gcéasadh do chine is do bhanúlachta
Is d'ealaíne
Go dtí sa deireadh
Gur scanraigh do ghuth féin tú,
A ainnir i sról.

BILLIE HOLIDAY

Pain you squeezed
From the ultimate sweetness
Sweetness
From the ultimate pain.
When you were raped –
Ten years of age –
That was the first nail
To pierce your people
To pierce your womanhood
To pierce your artistry,
Until in the end
Your own voice frightened you,
Lady in satin.

DOM SHEANCHARA, TOM GOGGIN

Mar go gcreideann tú i ngach rud
(Is níl aon rud ann)
Ní chreideann tú i rud ar bith.
Mar go gcreideann tú chomh láidir sin san oíche
Cuireann an lá díomá ort
Mar go gcreideann tú chomh láidir sin sa lá
Ortsa a thiteann oíche
Ach níl aon lá is níl aon oíche
Snámhann am
Snámh, mar sin ...
Snámh.
Gortaíonn bruacha mar nach bhfuil siad ann.

FOR MY OLD FRIEND, TOM GOGGIN

As you believe in everything
(And there is nothing)
You believe in nothing.
As your belief's so strong in night-time
The day must disappoint.
As your belief's so strong in daylight
On you night falls.
But there is no daytime, night-time –
Time swims.
So swim!
It is the riverbank that hurts –
Because it is not there.

DOM CHOMHFHILÍ

Tuigeann sibhse go maith
Nuair a théim ag iascach dánta
Chomh dócha lena mhalairt
Go ligim don iasc éalú!
Bronnaim oraibhse na héisc nár cheapas
Don lá a mbéarfaidh ocras oraibh ...

Tráth mheasas go raibh cearta iascaireachta ag cách.
Dá mbrisfí dorú ar dhuine againn
Nó dá gcaillfí baoite
Ná raibh le déanamh ach –
Ach chím anois nach amhlaidh atá.
Chím lorg buataisí sa láib
Nach n-aithním
Agus scáil ar an mbruach thall
Nach mbeannaíonn dom

Deasghnátha aonair i nglaise maidine.

TO MY FELLOW POETS

You are all well aware
that when I fish for poems
it's very likely that
I allow the fish escape.
I grant to you the uncaught fish
against your hungry days.

I thought once all had fishing-rights
and if one broke a line
or lost a bait
all he had to do was –
but things are not like that.

I see boot-tracks in the mud
I cannot recognize
and a shadow on the farthest bank
that does not raise its eyes.

In the morning's chill, these lonely rites.

KOAN

Mar go ngabhais thar bráid
Is mé go haclaí ag glanadh fiaile
Reoigh an spáid
I dtochailt na cruacheiste
Bhfuil dúchas an Bhúda ag gadhar?

Is ea is cinnte go n-áiteodh saoithíní orm
Cuimhneamh ar an tSalvadóir seachas scráid
Ar ghorta seachas gortghlanadh intinne
Ar dhiúracáin núicléacha seachas mo phaistese dúrabháin.
Ach nuair a ghabhais thar bráid
A ghadhair
Faoi thromshiúl daitheacha
Bhí freagra an tomhais agam láithreach.

KOAN

Because you passed by
When I, supple, cleared the weeds,
My spade froze
Digging the insoluble question:
Does a dog have Buddha's birthright?

It's certain pedants will persuade me
To contemplate San Salvador rather than turves
To contemplate famine rather than weeding my mind
To contemplate nuclear missiles rather than my patch of
  loam.
But when you passed by
My dog
With painful plod
I had the riddle's answer straight away.

DO MEG
(A chan i nGàidhlig,
oíche i Nua-Eabhrac)

An eol duit
nuair a chanais
narbh ann
níos mó
do na tithe spéire
gur líon
Nua-Eabhrac
le fraoch
le cuileann
gur iompaigh
tráchtghlór
ina phíobaireacht
nótaí binne
ag éag
i ngarbhchríocha
Manhattan
is bhíos
im bhuabhall
ar strae
i spás

FOR MEG
(Who sang in Scots-Gaelic
one night in New York)

Do you know
when you sang
nothing was
left anymore
of sky-scrapers?
That New York
was filled
with heather
with holly
that traffic-noise
was pipe-music
sweet notes
dying
in the highlands
of Manhattan
and I
was a buffalo
lost
in space.

AG FILLEADH AR AN nGÚM

A chairde geanúla,
Tá faolchoin ar na sráideanna
Tá siad feicthe agam le mo shúile cinn
Tá a ngeonaíl cloiste agam i gcorplár na hoíche
A scáthanna fiú is uafar
A dteachtaireacht is múisiam
Ag amhastrach leis an ngealach lán
Dearg na súl ag coimheascar leis an mbán.

A chairde geanúla, táim leonta,
Clúdaithe le cochaillí réama
Labhraíonn ulchabháin liom agus sciatháin leathair
Níl uaim ach sos tae... ag a haon déag... agus Ó!... ag a ceathair!

RETURNING TO THE GÚM

Beloved friends:
there are wolves on the streets –
I saw them with my own eyes.
I heard them howl in dead of night –
even their shadows terrify.
Their message is disturbing,
barking at the full moon
red eyes struggling with the white.

Beloved friends: I am wounded,
covered in phlegm-spittle.
Owls talk to me and bats.
All I need is a tea-break
at eleven
and – oh –
at four o'clock.

CAILÍN SCOILE I SÉIPÉAL

Pháirceáil sí a rothar ag doras an tséipéil
Agus shlog an dorchacht í (chomh hamplach leis an
  mbás).
An soilseoidh a hanam os comhair an taibearnacail
Nó an osclóidh sí a croí do naomh éigin
Faoi shearcrún (cuiream i gcás)?

An lasfaidh sí coinneal?
An ndíbreodh sin na scrúduithe as a cloigeann?

Samhlaím a dhá lámh, a dhá ghlúin le chéile
Samhlaím b'fhéidir méara solasmhara trí ghloine
  dhaite
Ar leathleiceann léi
Ar a bráid.

Cad a adhanfaidh Mac na hÓighe ar an gCrann inti
Na tairní
An ghoin ina thaobh geal
Féitheoga agus matáin?
An fínéagar a bhlaisfidh sí
Nó fíon?

SCHOOL-GIRL IN CHAPEL

She parked her bike at the chapel door
and the darkness swallowed her, greedily, like death.
Will her soul light up before the tabernacle
will she open up her heart to a certain saint –
about a secret love, perhaps?

Will she light a candle?
Will that banish examinations from her head?

I imagine her two hands, her two knees together
I imagine perhaps glowing fingers through coloured
  glass
on one of her cheeks,
on her neck.

What will the Crucifix kindle in her
the nails
the wound in Christ's bright side
the sinews and the muscles?

Will she taste vinegar
or wine?

PLANDAÍ BIALAINNE

Ní labhraíonn éinne
Leis na plandaí bialainne
Ní fheiceann siad grian
Ní bhlaiseann siad báisteach
Ceol gan stad
Ó stáisiún bradach
Amháin a chothaíonn iad
Ní theagmhaíonn freastalaithe leo
Faoina n-ualach bia dínádúraithe
Uaireanta, ámh,
I lár na hoíche
Síneann duilleoga ciúine
Chun Dé.

PLANTS IN A RESTAURANT

No one speaks to
Restaurant plants.
To see the sun,
To taste the rain? No chance.
Constant music
From pirate stations
Is their only sustenance.
The staff with their plates
Of foodless fodder
Do not grace them with a nod.
But sometimes, in the night,
Silent leaves stretch out
Towards God.

GIORRIACHA

Giorriacha ag pramsáil thar dhumhcha
B'in an méid
Ná bí buartha.

Leánn ar n-imlínte arís
Is gaineamh sinn
Is reiltíní
Is taoide aife.

Giorriacha sa mhuiríneach
B'in an méid
Ná bíodh imní ort.

HARES

Hares capering on dunes –
That's all.
Don't fret.

Our outlines melt once more,
Are sand
Stars
Ebbing tide.

Hares in the marram –
That's all
Don't be afraid.

UAMHAN

Scanraímid a chéile
Mar go bhfuil cumhacht againn ar a chéile
Tá de chumhacht ionam
Tú a chur ag snagaireacht
Tá de chumhacht ionatsa
Mé a iompú im
Pé ainmhí a fhreagraíonn dod bhrionglóid
Ag an am.
Míol mór bán tá súil agam
I nduibheagán do-eolais.

FEAR

Both frightened because
Each in the other's power.
I have the power
To make you weep.
You have the power
To translate me
To any creature
Answering your current dream –
A great white whale, I hope,
In unknown deeps.

RÚN NA gCAT

Tá na cait ag caoineadh arís anocht
Amhail is dá mbeidís i bpianta breithe
Is go raibh saol úrnua le cruthú as a dtocht –
Fáithe anois iad ag glaoch trí adharc reithe:
"Hósannah! Hósannah!" a chanaim i dtiúin leo
Ach teitheann na cait agus teitheann a rúin leo.

SECRETS

The cats are keening again tonight
as if they suffered the pains of birth:
as if new worlds came from their noise
they blow rams' horns and prophesise.
"Hosanna! Hosanna!" I sing in tune
but the cats take off – and their secrets too.

CLÉITHÍN

Ba gheall le mionsamhail
De dhealbh éigin de chuid Calder
An cachtas agat sa chistin,
Rian do bhanaltrachta ar a leathláimh leonta –
Cléithín!
Ní fhaca
Is ní dócha go bhfeicfead choíche
Cineáltacht mar é
Le ní briogadánach.
Dhoirtis grá
Is bhí an uile ní faoi bhláth.

SPLINT

It was like a miniature
of some sculpture by Calder,
your cactus in the kitchen.
It had signs of your nursing
on one broken limb –
A splint!
I never saw
(nor don't suppose I will)
such kindness
to a prickly thing.
You poured out love in that room
and every thing burst into bloom.

BÓ LASCAUX

A bhó ón anallód
Ar bhalla pluaise Lascaux
Nach giodamach ataoi
Tar éis tríocha míle bliain!
Cuid againne, a bhó, i gceann bliain nó dhó,
Cá bhfios an mbeimid ann níos mó?
A bhó bhuan bhithbheo na léime
Dúisigh led ghéim mé!

LASCAUX COW

Cow from an ancient age
on the wall of a Lascaux cave,
isn't it frisky you seem
after thirty thousand years!
Some of us, in another year –
who knows if we will still be here?
Immortal cow, with life glowing,
wake me someday with your lowing.

SCÁTHANNA

Ní féidir tú a phógadh, ní féidir!
ní féidir lámh a leagan ar fhíor na spéire!
ní féidir cur síos ar d'áilleacht ar phár
taoi gan imlíne, taoi gan lár.
Ár scáthanna ag súgradh lena chéile
gan sárú, a ghrá, gan géilleadh.

SHADOWS

I cannot kiss you, no, not I.
I cannot touch the edge of skies.
I cannot write about your splendour –
you have no border and no centre.
Our shadows, love, together playing,
no exhausting, no gainsaying.

SÉASÚR

seo an bhrionglóid
a bhí aréir aici
bradán sa leaba
gaoth an earraigh
ubh

brionglóid
a bhí agamsa
súil bhradáin
gaoth gheimhridh
deora Véineas am fhliuchadh

tharla go raibh dúil
ag an iasc sa réalt
cuirtear seo in iúl le scread ciúin

SEASON

this the dream
she dreamed last night
a salmon in the bed
spring wind
an egg

and a dream I dreamed
a salmon's eye
winter wind
tears of Venus drenching me

it happened that
the fish desired the star
this is revealed by a quiet scream

LAY OF AN OUTCAST INDIAN

AND they gave to us a desert
and our ancient gods went thirsty:
all our feathers lost their colours,
all the singing birds were silent.
No more the drone of falling water
wakes me as it did each morning –
here at journey's end I linger,
on strange windswept plains I linger –
of no cruel vows remind me.

MOTHER! Leave the pools to midges,
do not wash your breasts 'til doomsday:
all this stubborn land is rotten –
once a sun-bower for the nations.

MEAGRE soil they have allotted,
meagre, to inter our dead ones.
I am here where wind is howling
drinking dregs of vanished nations –
give me water out of pity,
give me strength to squeeze the cactus,

Granted rags to hide our bodies
temples fell, frost ate our totems –
flaying sun and taloned rainstorms,
snow-burnt buckskins, icy penance –
mother! where are my moccasins?

Strangers' language chokes us always
more than barren landscapes' dust-spews;
delicate now the dance and seldom –
who will word old lamentations?

Old men dribble free tobacco
– old tin cans now welcome spittle –
I long to rip it from their palates.
This soil's not ours, nor its products –
we are not the watchers of its
blossoms nor its cultivators.
Buzzard entrails, tails of rodents –
this is now our proper feeding.

I pray now at the sight of rainbows –
may the sun no longer scorch me,
may I not alive be buried,
may the gods not go unheeding
prayers of the wandering tribesmen.
But my plea is slang-polluted –
my voice is straw – I call on demons.

And my mother heard me talking
with a rattlesnake conversing
and in fear she cried out to me.
I search for life from blackest morning
search for life to blackest night-time
– way of life that no one practised –
whitest wand instead of hatchet,
all alone on empty prairies
and my booty's not for eating
and my booty's not for drinking –
though I share it no one sees it.

Once an omen came to tease us
came one day in mid-October –
wild geese honked about our wigwams.
And an ancient saw their coming
and hurried off to tell the wise men:
"Come out, come out, come, bestir you!"

and we stared at their wings beating
stared in awe at their wings beating –
warriors they were, off to battle
warriors they were, going hunting
or a conclave of the ancients
gathering their tribes for powwow.
One man fumbled with his quiver –
I in anger knocked him over:
"Oh my people, can you see not?
Our dead have sent these birds to free us."

But the world remained as always,
and the world remained in famine –
still the hate and spiteful spitting.
I still learn new incantations,
I understand the speech of pebbles.

Clouds and burnt-out skies have maimed me,
have gone straight into my marrow
and no flower grows that is not bitter
down among my soul's deep rootlets.
Dogs have breastplates made of gravel
too lazy now to scratch their vermin.
All the women's breasts are sagging
all their veins are over-swollen.
Now there is no thought of marriage
only thoughts of heavy burdens.
Piss flows freely, its steam is foglike,
mules hate the stench, add their portion.
The bald eagle in his heavens –
just one feather would mean freedom.

One sunny evening I decided
at last to finish my existence –
fact decided at my birthing.

I cannot imitate the others,
I shall not have the ghosts devour me,
I do not understand surrender.
I set out for distant places,
with a fist of poison berries.
On my way I heard coyotes
and the sun, it simply vanished.

In a fright I squeezed the potion
and so spilled the deadly juices –
I had to go back to my cabin,
my hair all nits that know no sorrow.

In labyrinthine night I ponder
long the cry of the coyote
speaking treason and retaken grass-lands,
it loosed a spasm of revolution:
I hear the buffalo stampeding
in my throat the smoke is stifling
I see the women violated,
I smell the stench-foretaste of Hades.

Wet sweat drowns me in its deluge
silken stings of my peyote
through my brain – so keep your distance!
Feverish wounds are self-inflicted,
threads are tearing, cold comes on me,
all my naked body changes
multicoloured mass of spirals
engraved with all the lore of deserts –
how the desert bloomed in old times.
Fat beavers they did lure the stranger,
catfish, trout and pollened clover:
change was brought by foreign violence,
lies and trickery stole our summer.

In a trance I then decided
to summon all things skeletal,
all the dead to call from graveyards,
tear them from their tombs to help me
plough the burnt plain of slaughter,
but they would not turn away from
pastures of Eternal Hunting.

And last winter we were saltless –
four braves died in the Big Canyon
in a fruitless search for tinder;
sorrow changed our childrens' faces
with sticks and bones they played grimly,
men spoke only when they had to
through the ancient womens' ravings.
Where's the laughter that will cure us?
Is it in my heart, this laughter?
Blistered heaven bleeds down pity.

Maize has failed again this season –
no sign of our promised Welfare.
Twenty went to New York city
and they stayed there, in that city
left behind among their people
just a broken-hearted vacuum.

Tonight a sudden sandstorm visits:
whisks the old tin can to darkness,
whisks away my peoples' vigour,
and the last lines of my poem.

DRY MARTINI WEEKEND

After the second one (a bottle)
I left them.
But they were still with me
Someone playing a slow piano –
blues from the early Twenties.
Fred probably –
Fred's the life and soul.
A crowd playing cards
a crowd tipsy, happy –
tired, exhausted, all of them
like a cigarette-end.
Bracelets, flanks,
false teeth.

In the bedroom
I tried to read.
Susanne in the bathroom
stripping off –
a glimpse of skin –
swimming-cap on head.
Steam.
Susanne's scent.
Eau-de-Cologne.

Suddenly
I am called.
Are they not gone yet?
Sons and Lovers
closed at page 265.
Spectacles back in my pocket.

'We know, Gabriel,
you're trying to study
but we heard . . .'
Yes, your Highness?
She looks around her.
'Not only is he clever
but he has a lovely voice as well!'
There is applause.
'Give us a song!' said the crowd.
Susanne looks at me
a glass on her knee,
all clean and sparkling.
'Fred, give us a hand.'
'If you please,' said the duchess.

Ich weiss nicht was soll es bedeuten

And ...
back again in the room.
I don't like the company.
Nor the music either.
I like Susanne, though:
I'd love to elope with her _
Friday, maybe,
before
the weekend of the Dry Martinis.

I OPEN MY POEM

I open my poem to bright things
in come oranges and dandelions
welcome
and sit down
and I'll be with you

Into my poem comes
a lovely snow-beaked cuckoo
welcome in

what is this?
a million gallons of sun

I open my poem to all that is
will be and was
or could be
error

now to me comes
an old cat
in its mouth a pigeon's leg
(such things have to happen)
well sit down awhile
mind that cuckoo
there's snow on its beak

find space for yourself
between
oranges and dandelions,
where do you hail from, old cat?
where's the rest of the pigeon?

I open my poem to creatures
alive and dead

and ivy comes in and brings
with it a wall
the wall falls on the cat
this is a tragic poem
in a way

somewhere in the world
a wall falls on a cat
a child

I open my poem again to bright things
but there is nothing
no bright thing left
and there's no point saying there is.

CLOCK

I put the clock in the fridge tonight
(People say I'm daft)
Clocks upset me,
make me deaf.
There is a certain tribe
(from God-knows-where)
who have not yet mastered Time:
yesterday is like
last year to them
(people say they're daft)
For example you might get
your long-dead grand-dad's
milk-bill there
but you can certainly
ignore it.
I put the clock in the fridge tonight
to prove some theory
which I can't recall.
The beet, the cheese, the frozen carrots
will wake at ten to eight.
Let them jump on a bus and take a ride –
I don't care:
I put the clock in the fridge tonight.

SOMETIMES I'M A LIAR

I

Sometimes I'm a liar,
I frighten myself –
my own lies torment me.

Strip my clothes from me,
tear them asunder.
Burn my entrails
'til I hear the pain-scream
of my birth.
I would walk through the world aflame,
I would speak in tongues of fire,
I would dance at fairs,
I would scare the children –
what would I not do!
I would leap to the sky as the Northern Lights
as a shooting star through the Milky Way.
Sometimes I'm a liar,
I frighten myself –
my own lies torment me.

II

Let the raven come
let him pick out my eyes –
I'd give a sickening laugh at wedding-feasts,
jump out of my skin at christenings –
I'd eat the green grass,
I'd drink hare's piss!
I am a liar
between heaven and earth –
blind to my destiny
I don't know the pedigree

94

of the furnace of my soul.
Sparks are released
from my eyes.
Sometimes I'm a liar,
I frighten myself –
my own lies torment me.

III

This skull no longer bothers me –
but leave my hat on me.
I'd go to be confirmed by the bishop
I'd rob the rings from his fingers
I'd buy a few loaves of bread
plus two salted herrings
and would wait for a miracle
or I'd simply perish.
Sometimes I'm a liar,
I frighten myself –
my own lies torment me.

IV

Who has tarred and feathered
my tongue?
Nonsense!
The wind will speak through me
for ever –
frosty tales
of travelling people
tales of fugitives and the homeless.
Sometimes I'm a liar,
I frighten myself –
my own lies torment me.

V

Take me to the river
the river Boyne
the Nile
dip me in the Ganges
or the river Jordan:
I have travelled through fire
through desert
through ice-floes
headless and faithful.
By God,
at last I demand a bank.

SOFT AND HARD

Opening his mouth
Chang Ts'ung said:
'See you?'
to Lao Tsu.

'I see,' said Lao Tsu.
Chang Ts'ung spoke:
'what see you?'

'I see your tongue,'
Lao Tsu did say
to Chang Ts'ung
who said 'Hurray!'

'But I see no teeth,'
said Lao Tsu.
'All gone, are they?
Poor you!'

Its own softness saved your tongue,'
said Lao Tsu to Chang Ts'ung,
'Your teeth's hardness left no tooth.'
Chang Ts'ung said, 'Forsooth!'

ONKEL OTTO

Oh Onkel Otto was well-fed as a pig!
Big cigars suited him.
A master baker.
None better in Schleswig-Holstein.
His cream cakes would make your eyes dance in
   your head.
All day he'd play sentimental music on a tape –
Du und ich
Und die Nacht
Und das Meer . . .
His wife, Tante Thea, put up with it all
Although she preferred *Oper* and classical music:
Oh *mein Bein, mein Bein* – my leg, my leg!
Poor hurt nightingale.
My job one summer was *Hände klatschen:*
To clap hands in the garden
To keep birds from the cherry trees.
That was easy.

At least it was easier than
Putting Onkel Otto and Tante Thea,
The music and cigars
The rooks, the cakes
And the cold cherry soup
Out of my mind.

TELEVISION
(For my daughter Saffron)

At five o'clock in the morning
she wants to watch the telly!
Can you argue with a little woman
two-and-a-half years old?
Down we went together –
I didn't bother dressing
and the room was perishing.
With no daylight in the sky
we watched in wonder the blank screen.
'Now! Are you satisfied?'
But she saw snow
and in the snow, giraffes,
and an Arctic owl
circling overhead.

HYMN

I yield to the smallest insect
I bow
I yield to the maggot
I bend my knee. Sing OM. Aililiú.
I yield to the oak and yew
I bow
to their sap
I bend my knee. Sing OM. Aililiú.
I yield to the new moon
I bow
I yield to the herb
I bend my knee. Sing OM. Aililiú.
I yield to the fox, to the badger
I bow
to hares and to hounds
I bend my knee. Sing OM. Aililiú.
I yield to the gannet
I bow
I yield without venom
I bend my knee. Sing OM. Aililiú.
I yield with ears and eyes
I bow
without fear or hate
I bend my knee. Sing OM. Aililiú.
I yield to the falcon
I bow
I yield to his cold talon
I bend my knee. Sing OM. Aililiú.
I yield to the wing and the claw
I bow
Full of love today
I bend my knee. Sing OM. Aililiú.

100

PURSUIT

I

Where are the poems I promised
I'd write for you?
They are not in print –
you will find them in river foam
in oceans
in wind on clifftops
in whirlwinds
in eagles' eyes
in clouds
in skies,
even in stars.
They go on their eternal round
from nothingness to nothingness.
They are not in print –
snatched by perfumed flowers
(you were on your hunkers
in the garden)
they were stung by nettles
caressed by dock leaves.
Lady-birds landed
and walked them like critics
seeking rhyme and metrics
not finding out the title.
You could not be named!
I acclaim you every day
with every breath.
Where are the verbs?
You have taken them to you.
The adjectives?
They nest in your breasts.

Punctuation?
You are adorned by it.
Noun, vowel and consonant,
every Gaelic sound,
Eithne, I dedicate to you.

II

From age to age I seek your form
I, a feather,
I, a leaf,
when we are children
warriors
ancients
about to die
or in the womb
each eternal moment
prepares my poem for you –
and welcomes you.
Do you hear a gale?
The world turns
all things turn,
the hills and mountains change.
We close, we open eyes
and close them again in wonder.

III

Do not greet me
do not look
do not seek me
I flee
to search for you.
There is no place

no time for us.
We are unbespoken
we are not in love
(strong as our mutual love is).
Take my hand my love
hear the heart's tambourine
that beat for us in ancient times –
we still don't understand its tune.

SHELLEY

'Shelley'
we called the terrapin,
the little fellow
with us a year he lived for a –
and fed on local insectivora.

One day when cleaning out his bowl.
in winter when his torpor is,
I put hot water in – a joke –
and what a metamorphosis!

His happy head he pushed outside:
'Am I in a tropic clime?'
I went out to the garden
and the first sod I turned
concealed a juicy worm.
But when I looked at him again
his mouth was wide, his eyes were dim –
most unusual for him!
Had I injured the poor thing?
I teased him and his flipper flipped.
Was he living yet?
There was a scum about his eyes –
had I boiled him alive,
my terrapin, my pet?

What to do, oh what to do!
Should I let him recover?
What did my nature say?
Smash his head in with a hammer.

"AND IF THINE EYE CAUSETH THEE TO STUMBLE, PLUCK IT OUT . . ."

I stared at a girl
across from me
on a station platform.
You know that stare,
often mentioned in womens' magazines.
I knew I was making her shy –
she pushed a tooth in her lower lip.
I was reading a book
on *literature engagée*.
Now and then I raised my head
my sharp and darting eyes
removed her every stitch.
The train was long delayed
and long her live act
on the cold platform –
long our double pain
and indivisible.

Oh lovely Christ
on the cross
I am the thief
you did not take
with you to Paradise.

SEA-HYMN

We, porpoises,
gambolling in sun
and glittering

the sea-bed envies us
the basking shark despises us
the jelly-fish would wound us
if we allowed it

cockles cleave to rocks
all aghast at us
lobsters fly in fear from us
sea-urchins, sea-snails
peevishly glance at us

gannets call raucously
in gravel turnstones
are gossip-mongers
the sea scorpion glowers at us
unseen things gurgle

We shall go to green seas far away

PHANTOM NEEDLES*

Never before did I see so many
Phantom Needles
It goes beyond me to explain
what they presage.

Their name scares me but
I must get used to it –
go under the skirts,
lie down with the language
even if a nightmare follows
even if shadows on walls
even if Phantom Needles
resound in my mind
and I become a fluttering thing
caught in their eerie capers.

(*Daddy long legs)

WOMAN IN WHEELCHAIR

Wheelchaired woman
moving through crowds,
turtle, slow-moving thing,
skilled in avoiding eyes
in your everlasting dusk,
won't you look up at us?
Won't you share with us
your chains?
Won't you allow the icebound streams
the summer trees
and heaven's stars
to raise you up?
– To look in wonder at yourself,
perfect in the light!

POETRY IRELAND
ÉIGSE EIREANN

The Organisation

Poetry Ireland organises readings by Irish and international poets throughout the 32 counties. We are supported by both Arts Councils in Ireland, by private and corporate sponsors, and by the general public. Members receive a bi-monthly Newsletter which gives details of readings, tours, lectures, competitions and services provided by Poetry Ireland. Poetry Ireland Choice is a subscription service which offers four collections of poetry each year to members, at a significant reduction in cost.

We also administer the Austin Clarke Library, a scholarly resource consisting mainly of the 6,000 volume collection built up by the late Austin Clarke.

Poetry Ireland Review

Poetry Ireland Review appears quarterly, and is sent automatically to members. Containing new poetry from Ireland and abroad, reviews, interviews and articles, the Review is now widely acknowledged as one of the liveliest and most challenging in the field.

MEMBERSHIP

We invite you to become a member of Poetry Ireland. Please clip and mail this coupon.

STANDARD MEMBERSHIP
I will receive bi-monthly Newsletter and four copies of
Poetry Ireland Review. ☐ $30

POETRY IRELAND CHOICE
I will receive four collections of Irish poetry ☐ $35

Books, Reviews and Newsletters will be sent air mail.

Name _____

Address _____

SEND TO: **The Director, Poetry Ireland, 44 Upper Mount Street, Dublin 2, IRELAND.**

POETRY IRELAND
President: John Montague. Chairman: Gabriel Rosenstock. Director: Theo Dorgan.

CELTIC DAWN

Published quarterly in the belief that poetry and other art-forms are integral to human existence.
Unique in publishing translations from many languages.

Editors: Dwina Murphy-Gibb, Terence DuQuesne, Chris Morgan.

No1 (Summer 1988)
Dance in Yeats's Theatre • Michael Field • Modern Poetry •
Yeats the Initiate • Fiction • Poetry • Reviews • Translations
from Greek, Egyptian, Irish, and Bengali

No 2 (Autumn 1988)
Gipsy Charms • Who was Sappho? • Poetry & Healing •
Brion Gysin/William Burroughs • Tom o'Bedlam • Poetry •
Translations • Short Stories • Reviews of Seamus Heaney,
Sylvia Plath, John Heath-Stubbs

No 3 (Spring 1989)
Karin Boye • Yeats & Femininity • Greco-Egyptian Magical
Papyri • Elémire Zolla • Poetry • Translations from
Swedish, French, Romanian, Italian, Danish, Gaelic • Short
Stories • Reviews of William Burroughs, Peter Redgrove •
Yeats Club Review

No 4 (Summer 1989)
Dino Campana • Bridie Morrigan • Hafiz • Justo Jorge
Padrón • Louis Aragon • Austin Spare
Competitions • Yeats • Re/Search • Ezra Pound • Magnus
Hirschfeld • Léopold Sédar Senghor • Runes & the Zodiac
by Elémire Zolla

Annual subscription: UK £10 post free. Europe & USA £14 (sur-
face mail). Individual copies £2.50 (UK), £3.50 (Europe & USA).

Prebendal Press Ltd, PO Box 30, Thame, Oxon OX9 3AD, UK

'Arguably the most exciting literary review in Ireland'

Published twice-yearly

John Arden	Thomas Kilroy
John Banville	Thomas Kinsella
Sebastian Barry	Michael Longley
Christabel Bielenberg	Thomas Murphy
Eavan Boland	John Montague
Eoin & Eva Bourke	John McGahern
Terence Brown	Tom MacIntyre
Harry Clifton	W. J. McCormack
Gerald Dawe	Dennis O'Driscoll
Peter Fallon	Cathal O'Searcaigh
Brian Friel	Liam O'Muirthille
Robert Johnstone	Frank Ormsby

Translations from Belgium; East Europe;
Interviews and Reviews

TRANSLATION ISSUE — AUTUMN 1989

From all good bookshops or direct from
Krino, Glenrevagh, Corrandulla, Co. Galway, Ireland.

Books Ireland is a magazine
supported by the Arts Councils of Ireland

11 Newgrove Avenue, Dublin 4

*we have our nervous breakdowns in January, July and August